NICK RITCHEY

Lean for Life

A Step-by-Step Guide to Weight Loss Mastery

For information about special discounts available for bulk purchases, sales promotions, fund-raising and educational needs, contact Nick Ritchey at Nick@LeanForLifeBook.com

Visit the author's website at www.LeanForLifeBook.com

First edition

ISBN: 9781081496944

This book was professionally typeset on Reedsy.
Find out more at reedsy.com

Contents

Download the Audiobook FREE!

Thanks for buying my book!

To show my appreciation, I would like to give you the Audio-book version 100% FREE!

DOWNLOAD AT:

www.LeanForLifeBook.com/Bonus/

About The Author

Nick Ritchey is a weight loss author, coach and speaker.

His fitness education began in 2008. In his search for a decent gym in London, he met Chris Young, who invited Nick to train at his home gym.

What looked like a simple shed on the outside, was a world-class facility on the inside. Responsible for forging national and world champions, like himself. Chris was a world champion powerlifter who trained professional athletes, celebrities, royalty... and now Nick.

They trained. Bonded. Grew stronger. And became best friends with shared interests.

After a year of training with Chris, Nick returned to Korea. Despite the distance, they continued to collaborate on projects. They published several books and started a podcast around skepticism, health and fitness.

The podcast was a hit.

With 5-star reviews and people coming out of the woodwork, it grew to over 150 episodes. Nick & Chris found themselves interviewing the best in the industry, including:

- Jill Mills – 2x World's Strongest Woman
- Ed Coan – The Greatest Powerlifter of All Time
- Nick Tumminello – *Strength Training for Fat Loss*
- Brian Carroll – *The Gift of Injury*
- John Little – *Body by Science*

And other amazing guests with inspiring stories. But the podcast didn't last forever...

Nick lost his youngest brother to pneumonia, and Chris to leukemia, in the same year.

For the first time in his life, Nick felt mortal.

But he felt compelled to make a positive dent in the universe. After picking the brains of the strongest men and women on the planet, Nick felt he had more to offer. But the clock was ticking...

So Nick got busy.

He spent the next 4 years combining his unique blend of theory and practice, including:

- 20 years teaching/coaching experience
- Personal success *(losing 80lbs & keeping it off since 2005)*
- Scientific understanding of human nature and behavior modification *(skipping 3 grades, B.Sci in Math, Master's in Applied Positive Psychology from UPENN)*

Into a comprehensive weight loss coaching program, bootcamp, and the book you have in your hands.

After life/travel in 20+ countries, Nick understands that "real-life is messy." So his program was designed to give anyone with the desire to get lean for life, the ability to make it happen... WITHOUT giving up the foods, friends, flexibility & fun – that make life worth living.

In 2018, after 14 years abroad, Nick returned to the USA. He's making up for lost time with friends & family. And continuing to make a positive dent in the universe.

To learn more about Nick's latest projects, visit LimitSlayer.com

Preface

"Nobody cares how much you know,
until they know how much you care."
–Theodore Roosevelt

This is the book I wish I had 20 years ago...

Before:

- Wasting $10,000+ on supplements
- Doing endless hours of crunches
- Fat burners, detoxes, superfoods
- Low-X diets (carb, fat, meat, sugar...)
- Wreaking havoc on my knees...

And the world of pain & declining self-confidence that come with it.

This book is the gift I spent YEARS preparing for my youngest brother. I was going to show him how I lost 80 lbs. How it transformed my life, the lives of my clients, and would improve his too...

I knew he silently struggled with his weight. But I was across the ocean in South Korea. Worlds apart... and I didn't have a step-by-step system developed yet.

It needed to be foolproof.

Not because he wasn't smart. Smart people struggle with weight loss ALL THE TIME. But because there are infinite ways to go wrong, and only a few ways to go right.

One day, when I moved back to the USA, the system would be perfected.

And I'd show him the ropes...

But I never had the chance.

My brother died young.

And overweight.

A few days after his 23rd birthday...

Friends have since died fat & full of problems. I've watched their health and happiness decline until some "crazy fluke" takes them suddenly.

But it's no fluke.

In general, heavier people die 2-20 years younger.

You're "lucky" if the downward spiral doesn't speed up.

My grandmother was one such "lucky" person. I watched her struggle with her weight my entire childhood. Well into her 80s — up until the day she died.

A slippery slope of declining health, confidence, mood and mobility is no way to live. As long as you're overweight, you're a slave to your excess fat.

We're all going to die...

But you don't have to live (or die) FAT.

The friends & family I mentioned didn't have a choice...

They didn't have this book.

But you do.

This book is my gift to you. Forged from years of sweat, blood & tears — it gives you an edge most dieters will never discover.

It can add years to your life, and life to your years.

But only if you let it...

I

The Journey to Lifelong Weight Loss

"If you deliberately plan to be less than you are capable of being, then I warn you that you'll be deeply unhappy for the rest of your life. You will be evading your own capacities, your own possibilities."
–Abraham Maslow

1

A F.R.E.S.H. Start

Continue or Change?

Are you sick & tired of being overweight?

And ready for a F.R.E.S.H. start?

If your **F**reedom, **R**elationships, **E**nergy, **S**ex & **H**ealth aren't where you'd like them to be, there's a tried & true way to fix them once and for all...

GET LEAN!

I know because I've lost over 80lbs.

Because it was the single greatest turning point in my life... I've spent the last 8 years sharing my "secrets" with friends, family & clients.

They've used these secrets to lose anywhere from 5 - 150lbs.

And now, I'd like to share them with you.

I say "secrets" because you'll find some of this content elsewhere...
But most dieters would be LUCKY to find 5% on their own.

This book can save you:

- Years or DECADES of dieting, rebounding & discouragement
- Thousands of DOLLAR$ in supplements, equipment & coaching.
- 2 - 20 years of life...

And it can breathe new life into your old ways.

These QUANTITIES (time, money, effort) are reason enough to get started. But the QUALITY of life you'll experience...

- More Freedom

- Better Relationships
- Abundant Energy
- Amazing Sex
- Superhuman Health

These are the REAL reasons to look forward to a F.R.E.S.H. start.

Imagine...

(F)reedom from excess body fat

No more carrying around excess fat which makes your joints ache, and your heart sink.

Better (R)elationships from the halo effect

By getting lean, people will think the "new you" is smarter, sexier & more successful. People like people whose fat doesn't invade their already cramped airplane seats...

Abundant (E)nergy

Your excess body fat is like a weighted vest you can't take off. For me, it was a vest which increased my weight & girth as much as 80lbs of mayonnaise...

If you strapped on an 80lb vest:

- Would you sweat while going up stairs?
- Would your back and knees hurt?
- Would it be hard to stand up and sit down?

You bet!

Now imagine, you take that 80lb vest off...

How do you feel?

- Light, free and unburdened?

7

- Happy, healthy and terrific?!

When you shed unwanted fat, your body breathes a sigh of relief!

You discover ENERGY you never knew you had!

Better (S)ex.

When you forge a better body you can be proud of, you look, feel & move better. You're more confident, energetic and desirable. You're more fun with clothes on AND off...

(H)ealth comes easier & stays longer.

Almost without exception, getting leaner adds years to your life, and life to your days.

You can have a F.R.E.S.H. start and more...

But first, a word of CAUTION.

If you're on a downward spiral, this trend doesn't reverse itself. And if it continues, you'll likely experience:

- Guilt, shame & self-doubt
- A harder time losing weight
- Greater risk of depression
- An expanding waistline
- Declining health

· Physical pain

And a shorter life.

But the trend doesn't need to continue...

The body & life you've always wanted is a short read away.

Will today be a turning point you remember for the rest of your life?

Or one you forget on the road to, "How the hell did I get here?"

If you flip the page, you won't regret it.

But the choice is yours.

Choose wisely.

"You are not your body and hair-style, but your capacity for choosing well. If your choices are beautiful, so too will you be." –Epictetus

2

The 4 Stages of Weight Loss

"When we are no longer able to change a situation,
we are challenged to change ourselves."
-Viktor Frankl

Well done!

You made an excellent CHOICE to continue. Now it's time to hold up my end of the bargain, and get you lean for life.

If you've struggled to lose weight in the past, it's likely because you didn't know where you were on the journey...

And got lost.

Here's your map.

You can remember it as "You See, I See."

With it, we can discuss the journey to lifelong weight loss.

The UCxIC in "You See, I See" stands for:

- Unconscious - unaware
- Conscious - aware
- Incompetent - unskilled
- Competent - skilled

And forms the "4 stages of competence" in skill acquisition:

- Outsider – Unconscious Incompetence (UI)
- Novice – Conscious Incompetence (CI)
- "Success" – Conscious Competence (CC)
- Master – Unconscious Competence (UC)

If you're wondering, "Why are we discussing skill acquisition?"

You're not alone.

This "wondering" is the #1 reason dieters fail. Most people don't see weight loss for what it really is...

Weight loss is a SKILL.

And this is why we're discussing skill development.

In 1969, Martin Broadwell proposed all skill development goes through 4 stages (above). If weight loss is a skill, and all skills go through these stages, weight loss goes through the same stages.

Once you realize this, everything changes.

Instead of being a slippery, confusing, mishmash of pseudoscience & hope...

Weight loss becomes a clear & concrete skill ANYONE can learn.

Map in hand, let's take a big picture view of the journey...

3

Stage 1 - Outsider

"Until you make the unconscious conscious,
it will direct your life & you will call it fate."
–Carl Jung

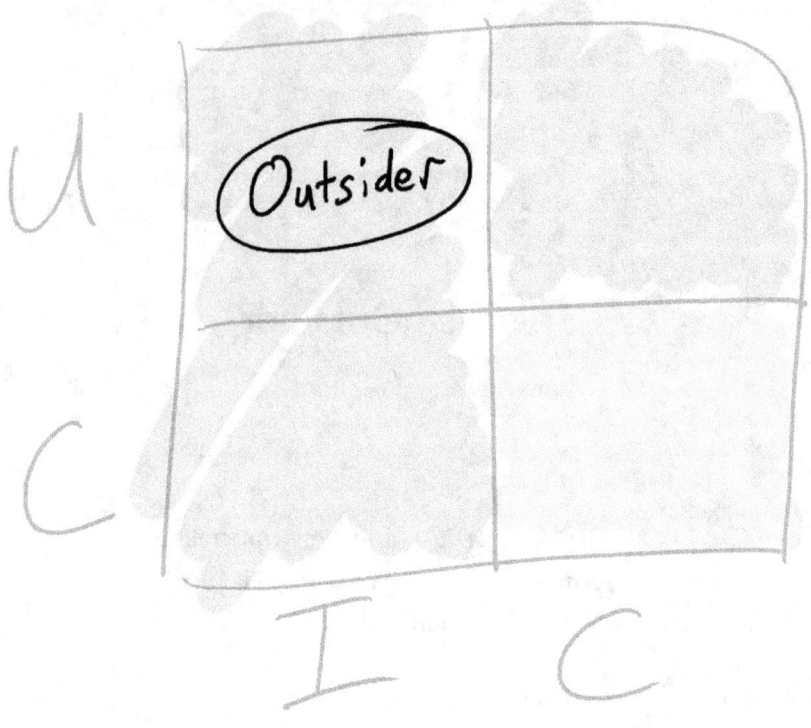

You're overweight & unaware weight loss is a skill.

- Not a genetic failure
- Not a moral failure
- Not a lack of intelligence or willpower

And DEFINITELY NOT your FATE!

It's just a skill.

Like playing chess, an instrument, or practicing a martial art. It comes more naturally to some than others. You're one of the "others."

An outsider.

Your excess body fat is sucking the life out of you. But you don't realize it.

Not yet.

It's not painful enough to register on your radar. To see through the cloud of denial...

Then one day, the scales tip.

Inaction becomes more painful than action.

So you decide to act.

What comes next is critical.

4

Stage 2 - Novice

"Honesty is the first chapter in the book of wisdom."
–Thomas Jefferson

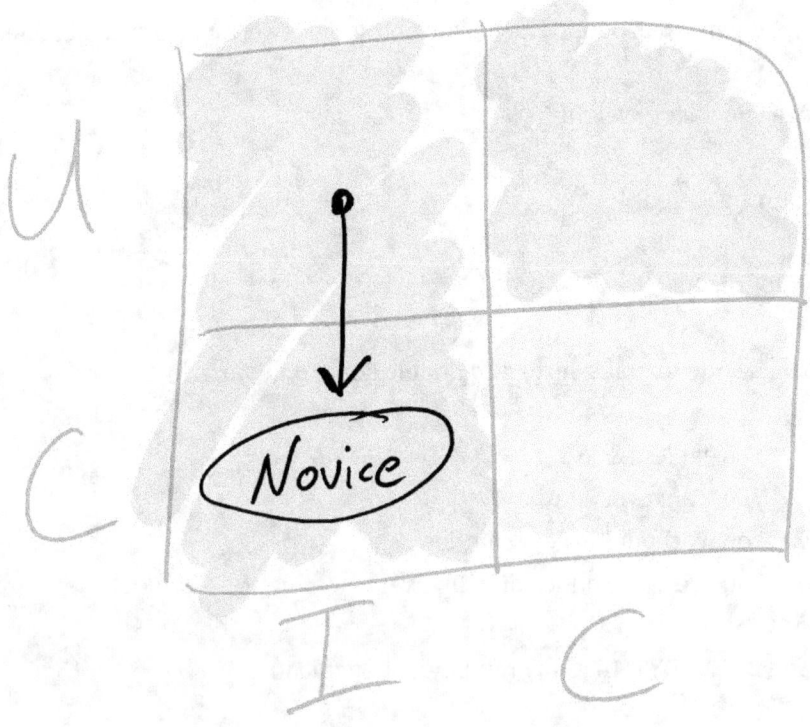

You realize you're overweight, and decide to do something about it. You do your research. Decide on a course of action.

Then it begins.

You start working your butt off.

- Week 1 – Lose 5 lbs
- Week 2 – Lose 3 lbs
- Week 3 – Lose 2 lbs
- Week 4 – Lose 1 lb
- Week 5 – Nothing...

Up, down, all around. The needle on the scale becomes unpredictable.

Are you losing weight?

Gaining weight?

What the hell?!

You decide to make sure. And double down on your efforts.

- You eat less & less.
- You train every day.
- You workout harder & harder.
- You use every ounce of willpower.

And do EVERYTHING in your power to get lean...

Nothing.

You're leaner than when you started. But you're tired, frustrated, and KNOW you can't keep up the pace. It hasn't even been 3 months...

How on earth will you get, let alone STAY lean for life?!

Either you make a comfortable EXCUSE to give up. Like "bad genetics" or "it's not worth it." Or you realize what most people don't...

Hard work & determination are NOT enough.

Imagine a novice boxer stepping into the ring with a pro. Even if the novice "wants it more" and "gives it 110%" there's only one outcome...

The novice gets knocked on his ass.

To beat the novice, the pro doesn't need to care. Or even try... because the pro has something the novice lacks...

Skill.

Many lean people learn the skills of weight loss from birth. A special combination of nature and nurture. They develop unconscious competence without ever trying or even thinking about it...

How anyone struggles with weight is a complete mystery to them. The first idea which comes to their mind is, "Fat people must be stupid." And it sticks.

Hence the stereotype.

Lucky them. But you're not them. You're a novice. Nature didn't do you any special favors. The only way for YOU to get lean for life is to be like the pro boxers...

Improve your skill in weight loss, or you don't stand a chance.

5

Stage 3 - "Success"

"Nothing will work unless you do."
–John Wooden

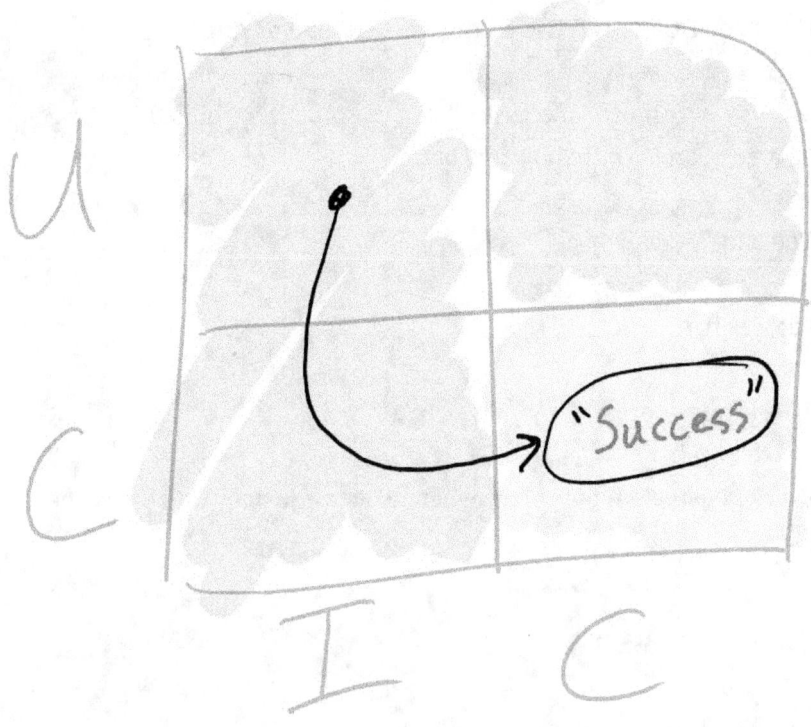

You've learned a ton about weight loss. Applied your knowledge. Increased your skills.

And now, your body reflects your learning.

It's leaner, stronger, and healthier than ever.

You're in the "success" phase.

You LOVE yourself.

AND your body.

What you DON'T LOVE is all the work it takes to stay lean...

This is where most "successful" dieters stop. They think this is as good as it gets, and don't know any better.

Too bad.

Fat was hell.

This is purgatory.

Don't get stuck in purgatory when heaven's just around the corner.

6

Stage 4 - Master

"Start by doing what's necessary.
Then do what's possible; suddenly
you're doing the impossible."
–St. Francis of Assisi

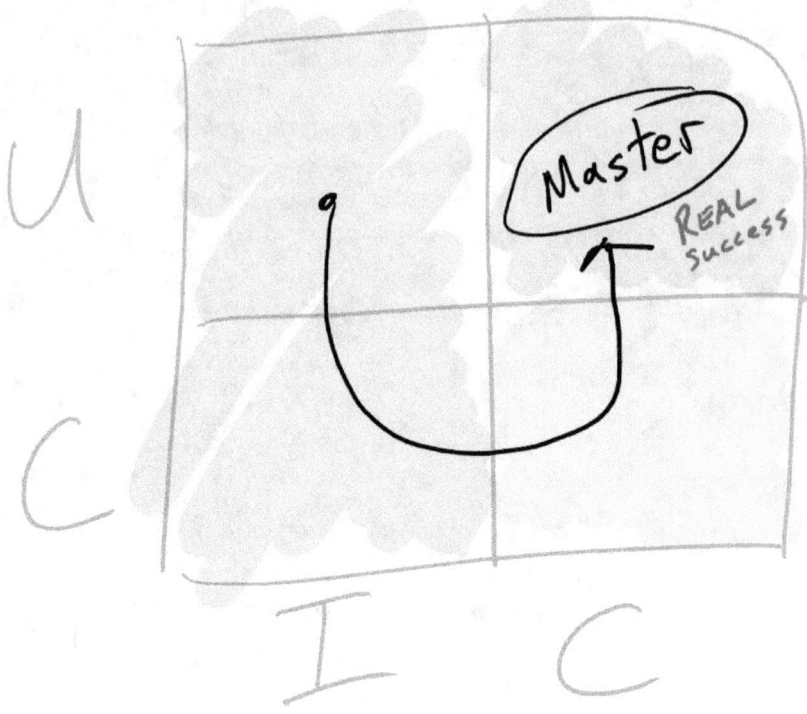

I'm assuming your goal is to develop unconscious competence in weight loss. To become a weight loss master, where being lean is:

- Easy and automatic.
- A way of life.
- Second nature.

If so, you have the right goal...

But there's a HUGE gap between learning some Spanish in high school, and becoming FLUENT in Spanish. Between being able to read sheet music, and becoming a concert pianist. Between moving the chess pieces, and becoming a grandmaster.

And this difference is why most "successful" dieters are FAILURES in disguise.

The problem is, most dieters stop at "success." Where, to stay lean, they have to work HARD for the rest of their lives. When they get old or injured...

They're screwed.

The weight comes back. And because they can't work as hard anymore, they either give up, or fight a losing battle until the day they die.

Tragic.

But it doesn't have to be this way...

Instead, you can continue increasing your skills. Getting better and better at weight loss. Making it easier & easier to stay lean. Having more & more fun...

Until one day, you're a master.

A weight loss "**BlackBelt.**"

So tell me...

Would you rather work hard for the rest of your life to stay lean?

Or get so damn good at being lean, it becomes second nature?

It's a simple choice.

An easy choice.

A real no-brainer...

So why don't more people get to weight loss BlackBelt?

7

One Journey, Many Traps

"If you don't see a sucker at the table, you're it."
–Amarillo Slim

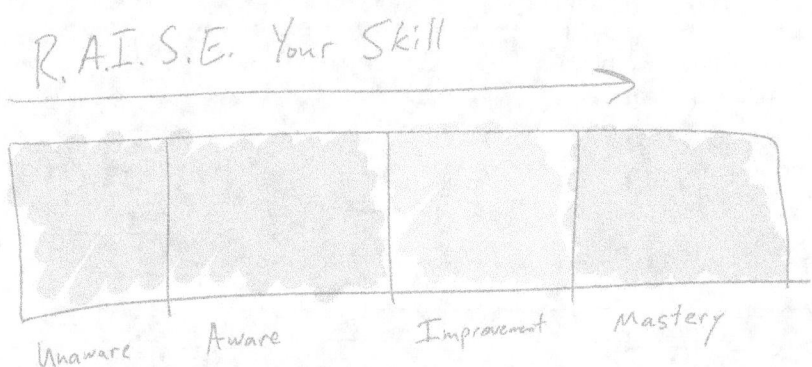

The journey from novice to master is wonderful, but dangerous.

Novices WANT to get lean.

But most don't realize:

- **Weight loss is a SKILL**
- And their <u>skill is LOW</u>

So they:

- Look for quick-fixes
- OVERESTIMATE their abilities (Dunning-Kruger effect)

And <u>DEMAND the impossible.</u>

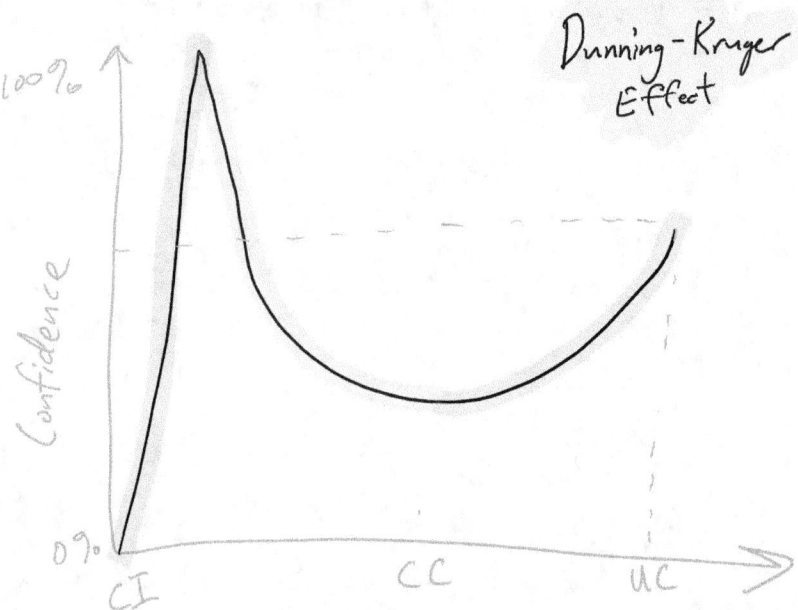

The Dunning-Kruger effect creates a unique combination of <u>confidence WITHOUT competence.</u>

28

Novices WANT to be lean. And think it will be easy.

But they're not good at discerning the gold from the garbage. Their expectations are HIGH. And from basic economics, we know when there's high demand, supply will rise to meet it.

Want eternal life?
  Go to church.

Want to reverse aging?
  Buy "anti-aging" creams.

Want to know your future?
  Find a palm reader, astrologer, or stock broker...

When people demand something, <u>they get it.</u> In exchange for their hard-earned cash.

<u>Even if it's impossible...</u>

In weight loss, the demand is, "I want to get lean without changing anything."

But Einstein says, "The **definition of <u>insanity</u>** is doing the same thing over and over. Expecting different results."

When novices make insane demands, they get insane solutions.

And pay through the nose for them in the form of:

  · The latest fad diet

- Fat shaking belts
- Weight loss pills
- "Detox" diets
- Pyramid schemes
- Weight loss acupuncture
- Psychic surgery
- Etc.

The list goes on and on...

See WhatsTheHarm.net for a small $2.8 billion dollar list of crazy solutions to insane demands. I know, I'm not making any friends here... but if you've ever secretly wondered if the whole weight loss world is crazy...

You're not alone.

In fact, the scary thing is... you're right.

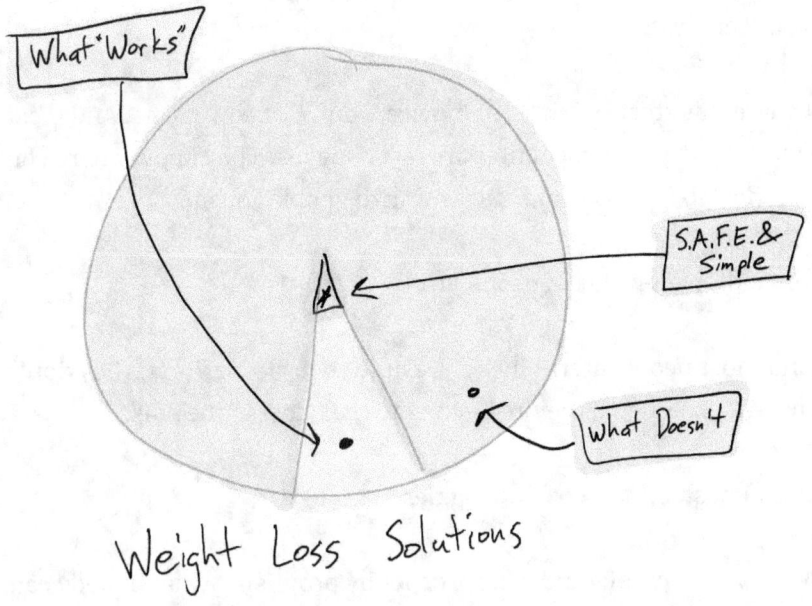

In the first episode of "Planet Earth 2," there's an amazing scene.

A baby iguana is sitting on the rocks... watching as a racer snake comes inches within its face. Knowing through instinct that if it doesn't move, it should be OK.

The snake passes by.

But another is right behind it. And bumps into baby iguana... so much for stealth. The iguana explodes into a sprint...

Followed by HUNDREDS of racer snakes!

To finish the story, type "iguana vs. racer snakes" into YouTube.

You'll enjoy it.

I share this story because as a novice, you're a baby iguana. And most "solutions" you'll encounter are racer snakes. They know where you are, how to find you, and are waiting to gobble you up.

You either get lucky, or get eaten.

And most people aren't lucky. Despite their best efforts, they don't make it. The signal they're looking for gets lost in the noise.

The honest, ethical coach struggles.

Meanwhile, crooks and cons prosper by promising what nobody can deliver. Crazy solutions to impossible demands.

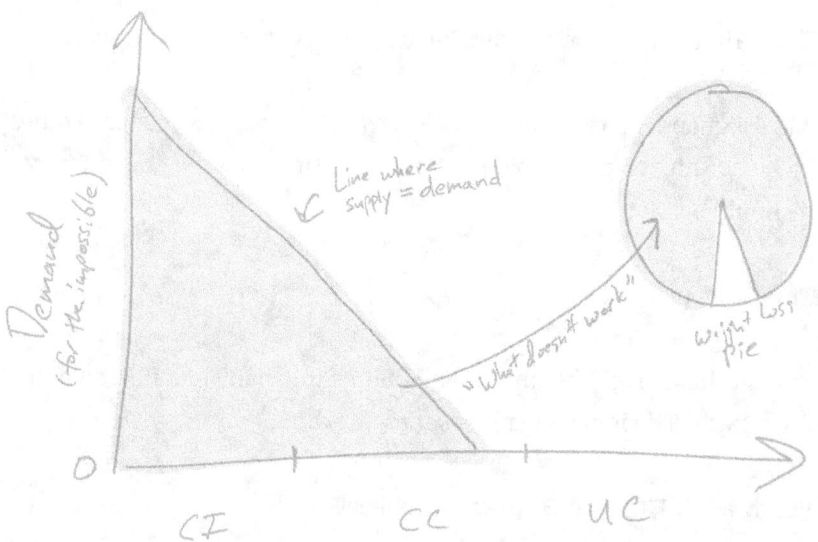

But somehow, you found this book.

And with it, you'll learn who the predators are, and how to avoid them. What the nonsense is, and how to avoid it.

There's hope.

As you increase your skill in weight loss, you'll make more realistic demands. Unlike impossible demands with no solution, realistic demands have real solutions.

Solutions that WORK.

And when you start working with reality instead of against it, you start getting REAL RESULTS. By increasing your skill in weight loss, you:

- Avoid getting eaten by snakes
- Take luck out of the equation
- Give yourself a F.R.E.S.H. start

And get lean for life.

Here's the S.A.F.E. & Simple way to make it happen.

8

R.A.I.S.E. Your Skill in Weight Loss

"In every affair consider what precedes & what follows.
Then undertake it."
–Epictetus

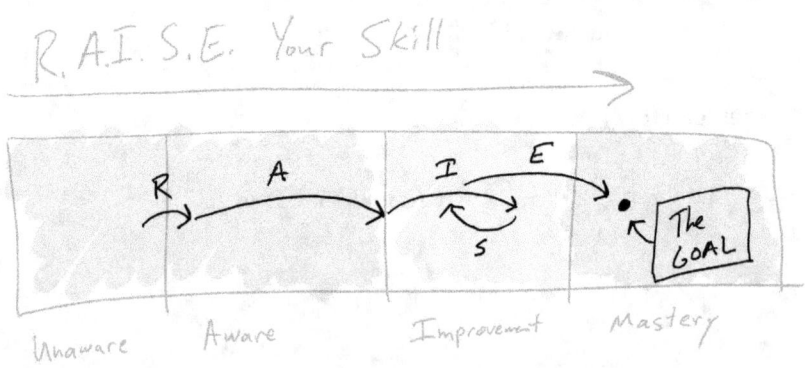

As you R.A.I.S.E. your skill in weight loss, you pass 5 milestones:

· (R)ealization

- (A)ction
- (I)mprovement
- (S)tagnation
- (E)volution

Think of each as a belt you earn on your journey to Weight Loss BlackBelt.

- Each signifies progress.
- Each has its own tests.
- And each is cause for celebration.

The only way you'll fail is if you quit.

> *"Quitters never win and winners never quit."*
> *-Jim Rohn*

Realization

You're no longer unaware/delusional about the fact that you NEED to lose weight. You acknowledge it. And know life will be better when you're lean. You just need to figure out HOW to get there...

Action

You don't daydream about getting lean. You DO something about it. Act too soon, or on the wrong information, and you're in for a heap of trouble. But do the right things in the right way, and your actions bring...

Improvement

You start looking & feeling better. You enjoy the initial results and are hungry for more. But diminishing returns kick in. In time, you experience...

Stagnation

Your weight loss comes to a screeching halt, or worse. You may gain a little weight back, or a ton with a vengeance.

Fear sets in.

It's fight or flight. Here is where many pack up their bags, and go home. Others spin their wheels, and go nowhere in the mud.

Not you.

You're going to fight. And you're going to win. Because you know weight loss is a skill. So there's only one thing to do...

Take your skills to the next level.

As you do, you get leaner than ever, easier than ever.

And the result is...

Evolution

You've mastered the basics to the point of unconscious competence. Being lean is easy & automatic. You're a Weight Loss BlackBelt:

- Free from the fear of weight regain
- Looking and feeling better than ever
- Able to enjoy food, friends & fun without blowing up like a balloon

Your confidence & competence act as a springboard for success. Because once you realize you can change your body, you realize you can change life.

You continue to evolve, and discover life without limits.

- (R)ealization
- (A)ction
- (I)mprovement
- (S)tagnation
- (E)volution

These are the 5 milestones on your journey to weight loss mastery.

Now that you've seen the big picture, it's time to dive into the details. We'll go through each stage of the journey step-by-step, so you know exactly what to expect...

And how to move to the next milestone.

This book is brief, so you can read it in one sitting. In less than the time it takes your friends to watch a movie, you can get the keys to lifelong weight loss.

Then, as soon as you put this book down, you'll be ready for action.

Let's begin with the end in mind (milestone 5) so we can reverse engineer success.

II

The "What" of Weight Loss

"Only the educated are free."
−Epictetus

9

Milestone #5: Evolution

"It is said the warrior's is the twofold Way of pen and sword, and he should have a taste for both Ways. Even if a man has no natural ability, he can be a warrior by sticking assiduously to both divisions of the Way."
–Miyamoto Musashi

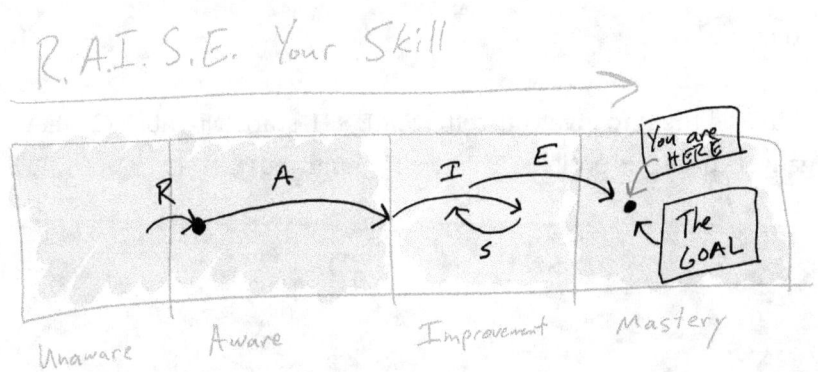

Poor Bob.

He's all excited about his new diet. He's losing weight and loving it.
But you politely bite your tongue because you know it won't last...

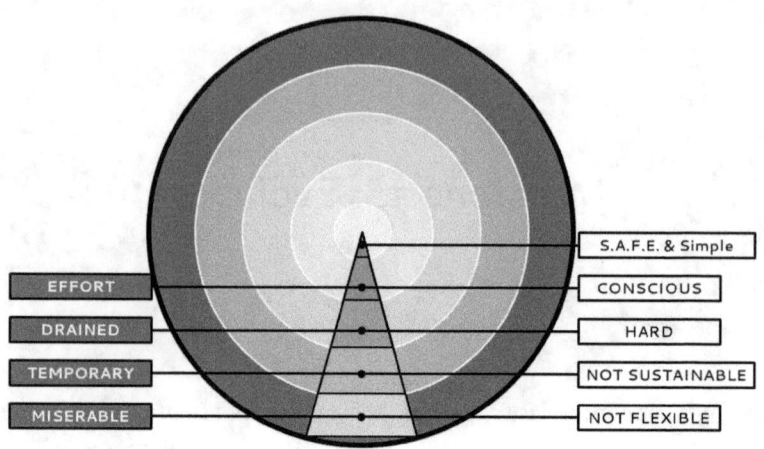

You'd like to help, but your words can't reach him right now.

Bob has a sword (action), but no pen (wisdom).

You have both.

You used them to give yourself a F.R.E.S.H. start. No more fad diets,
gadgets or magic potions. That's all behind you.

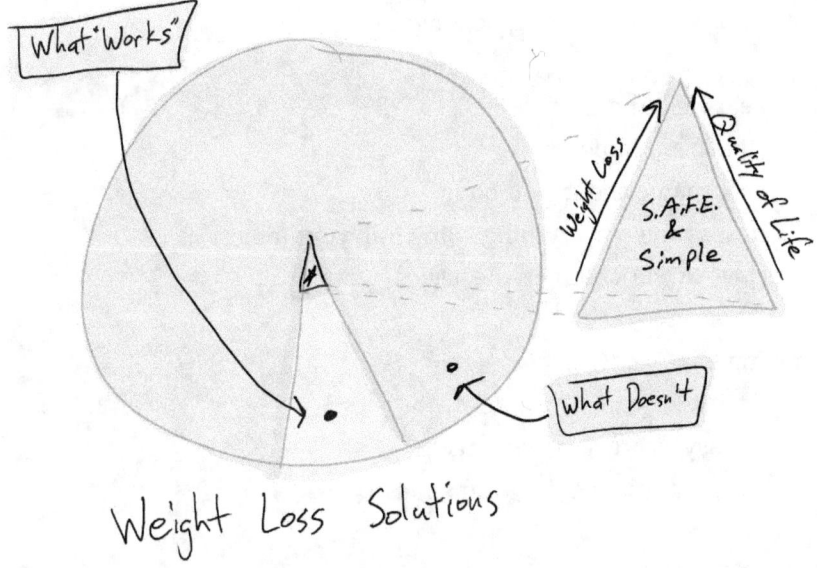

The changes you made are S.A.F.E. & Simple:

- **S**ustainable - so the fat stays off
- **A**utomatic - so you don't have to think about it
- **F**lexible - so you can live each day to its fullest
- **E**asy - so you don't struggle to stay lean

And **SIMPLE.** Because clarity is power.

If everyone could see what you could see, they'd **STOP**:

- Killing themselves in the gym
- Swearing off their favorite foods & drinks
- Beating themselves up for making mistakes
- Running away from fun & rewarding social lives
- And over-complicating what, in truth, is a set of simple life **skills**.

You're a WL BlackBelt and <u>no longer</u>:

- Fear weight regain
- Hide from cameras
- Feel shame about your body
- Obsess about everything going into your mouth
- Have to work hard on the basics

Staying lean is now:

- As easy as brushing your teeth
- As automatic as tying your shoes

But FAR more rewarding.

Life is good.

And it all began with a realization...

"Evolving is life's greatest accomplishment & its greatest reward." –Ray Dalio

10

Milestone #1: Realization

Realization: n. an act of becoming fully aware of something as a fact

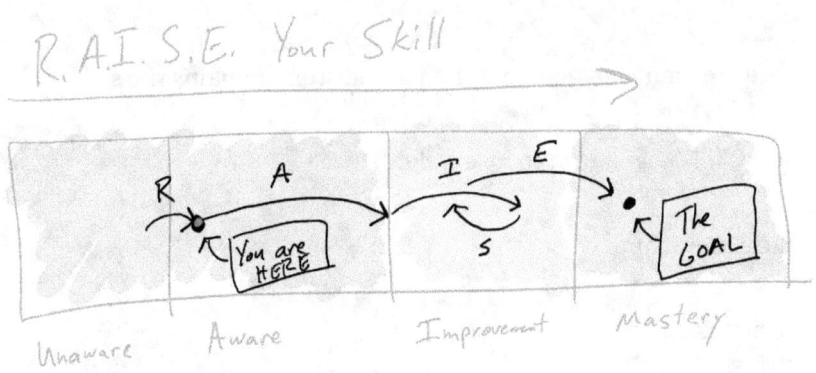

R.A.I.S.E. Your Skill

R   A   I   E

You are HERE   S   The GOAL

Unaware   Aware   Improvement   Mastery

Congratulations!

You've had an awakening.

And passed the first milestone of your weight loss journey. You've gone from outsider to novice by <u>REALIZING</u> you need to lose weight.

For some people, it's surviving a major medical event. Your doctor tells you you're lucky to be alive. But if you want to stay alive, you need to lose weight.

Maybe you have a new baby on the way. You want to be a good role model, AND have the energy to play with them.

Perhaps you stepped on the scale recently, and noticed your weight is at an all-time high. And you DO NOT want the trend to continue.

Or one day, you were HORRIFIED by what you saw in the mirror... or a recent photo.

"My GOD! How did this happen?!"

There are many triggers, but the 1st milestone remains the same.

You <u>REALIZE</u> you need to lose weight.

Take a moment to celebrate.

Because many people never get here.

Denial is too strong.

Reality is too harsh.

Friends & family are too "kind" to tell them the truth. So they stay asleep and continue gaining fat until it buries them in an early grave.

Not you.

You're awake, and ready for action!

11

Deciding to Act

"No man is free who is not master of himself."
–Epictetus

After your realization, you decide to embark on the journey to lifelong weight loss.

At this point, you're unaware of the dangers.

So it's hard to guard against them.

People used to:

- Eat tapeworms for weight loss
- Smoke for health

And put radioactive products on their faces for youthful beauty...

Dangers abound — but they're often hiding in sheep's clothing.

Often you'll find a fellow friend, family member or colleague doing something crazy. They'll be full of motivation & loving it. Love is blind...

And they'll blindly try to recruit you.

Just like the early adopters of smoking and radioactive facial creams...

New is not necessarily better.

And fads come and go.

For now, forget about them. And other shiny objects.

Instead, focus on what always has and always will work.

It begins with a few simple questions:

- Where are you now?
- What needs to improve first?
- What will you do when motivation wanes?
- How will you make your changes enjoyable and lasting?

These are the questions we'll answer in the following pages.

How YOU put them into practice will vary from everyone else. Depending on your personal circumstances. But when you do, people WILL take notice.

And ask how you did it.

When they do, you can share the following...

12

Milestone #2: Action

"First say to yourself what you would be;
and then do what you have to do."
–Epictetus

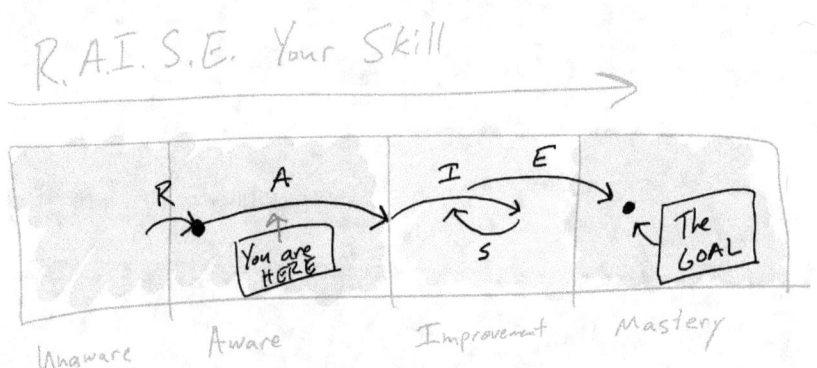

I know, you CAN'T WAIT to act!

But before jumping out of the plane, let's make sure you:

- Have a parachute
- And it's strapped on right

You can speed up your weight loss by weeks, months, years (even decades) with this short book...

But you can also experience slow (or no) progress because you're doing the wrong things in the wrong ways.

Here's your map for lifelong weight loss.

13

Mind the Gap

"Don't get involved in partial problems, but always take flight to where there is a free view over the whole single great problem, even if this view is still not a clear one."
–Ludwig Wittgenstein

There's a gap on the journey between novice and master.

This is how you bridge it:

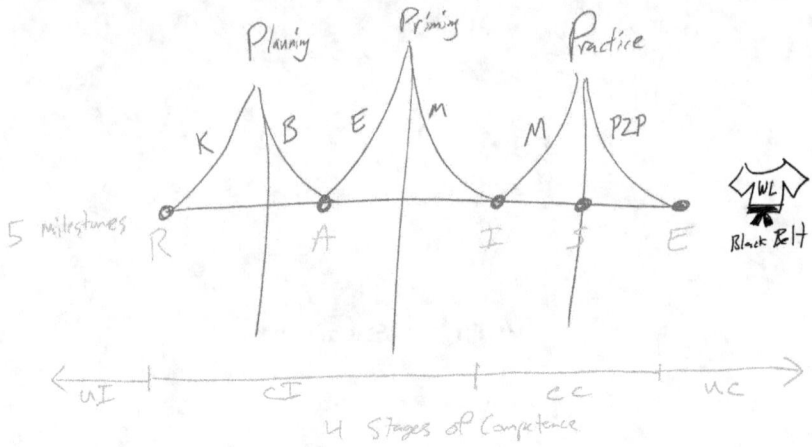

There are 3 pillars and 6 cables which support your journey to weight loss BlackBelt. In bootcamp, we spend one week on each:

1.Planning

- (K)nowledge – WHAT to do.
- (B)lueprint – HOW to do it.

2.Priming

- (E)ngineering – Your physical game. How to make it easy to succeed & hard to fail through environmental engineering.
- (M)indware – Your mental game. How to make it easy to succeed & hard to fail with mental (re)programming.

3.Practice

- (M)astery - Practicing the skills that make & keep you lean.
- (P2P) Pain to Power - Turning pain & plateaus into power.

My members get this in video form because it's quicker, easier to consume and more efficient than a book. Converting everything to book form would take at least 2000 pages...

And FOREVER to read...

It would be like trying to open a coconut with your teeth... it just doesn't make sense. So instead, let's cover the most impactful ideas in book form.

By leveraging the Pareto Principle (A.K.A. 80/20 rule) for weight loss...

We'll focus on the 80/20 of the 80/20 of the 80/20.

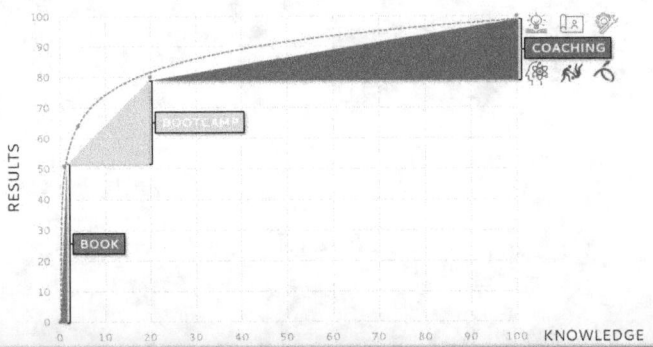

LEAN FOR LIFE 80/20 PROGRESSION

We'll cover the 1% of knowledge which give you 51% of results.

In practice, this means you can get lean doing very little.

Pretend you're a contestant on the show "Biggest Loser." To lose the average of 4.3lbs a week, you will exercise 4-6 hours PER DAY.

Who has time for that?!

Probably not you, and definitely not me.

It's unsustainable.

And a big part of why so many contestants gain the weight back. But given these numbers, the 80/20 principle predicts you could lose 2.15lbs a week in just 3 minutes/day.

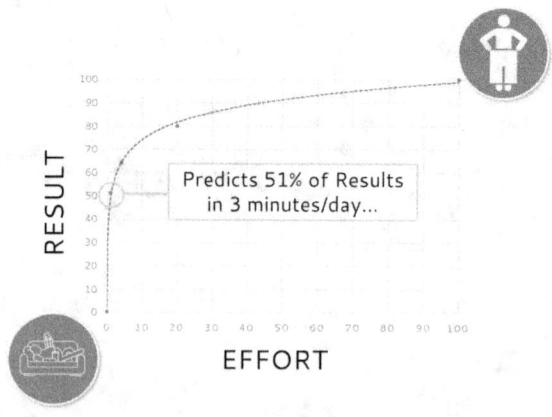

If more contestants knew they could make HALF the progress of their peers in just 3 minutes/day...

They'd walk right off the set.

And in my experience, 3 minutes is about right...

It doesn't take a lot to get a 400lb person losing 2.15lbs a week. That's about 1/2 of 1% bodyweight. Easily attainable, even if you're already lean.

True, they won't look as good as the winner...

BUT they will:

- Have an easier time getting lean
- Keep the weight off

And look a hell of a lot BETTER than when they started.

What about you...

How lean do you want to get?

Depending on your goal, this is what it takes to get there...

You can expect to look:

- AMAZING (80%) in ~1 hour/day
- Good (64%) in ~15 minutes/day

And a hell of a lot better (51%) in ~3 minutes a day.

We're skipping 100% because competition bodybuilding prep is a horse of another color. Riddled with drugs, eating disorders and a host of physical and psychological maladies...

It's not my thing.

I help people look AND feel better...

NOT become deathly ill while trying to look like anatomy models.

So in this book, we'll focus on the 1%.

Going beyond the 1% is mostly a matter of doing more of the same, with diminishing returns. So you can go there if you want. And if you're still itching for more at the end of this book...

I'll give you the shortcut.

So you don't have to read 99 books to pick up the remaining 49%.

Fair enough?

If so, let's dive into the 1%.

14

The 1st Pillar: Planning

"Fail to plan and you're planning to fail."
–Benjamin Franklin

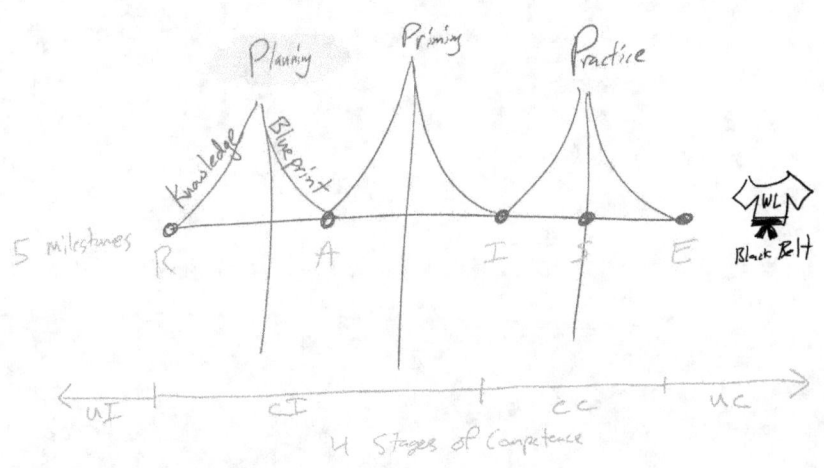

Planning has 2 parts:

- Knowledge - WHAT you need to know
- Blueprint - HOW to implement it

In this section you'll discover:

- Your 4 blind spots
- How weight loss works
- The 5 skills which make & keep you lean
- The importance of getting to weight loss "baseline"
- Your step-by-step blueprint for success

We'll start by shedding a light on your blind spots.

15

Knowledge: Your 4 Blind Spots

"Knowing what thou knowest not is in a sense omniscience."
–Piet Hein

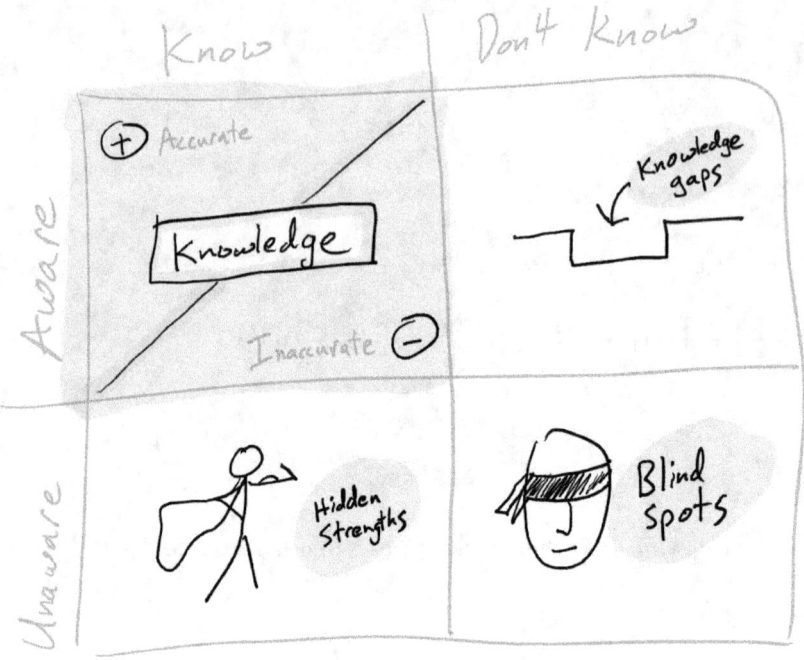

To become a weight loss BlackBelt, you need to overcome 4 blind spots.

These are...

1. KNOWLEDGE

These are the things you're AWARE you KNOW.

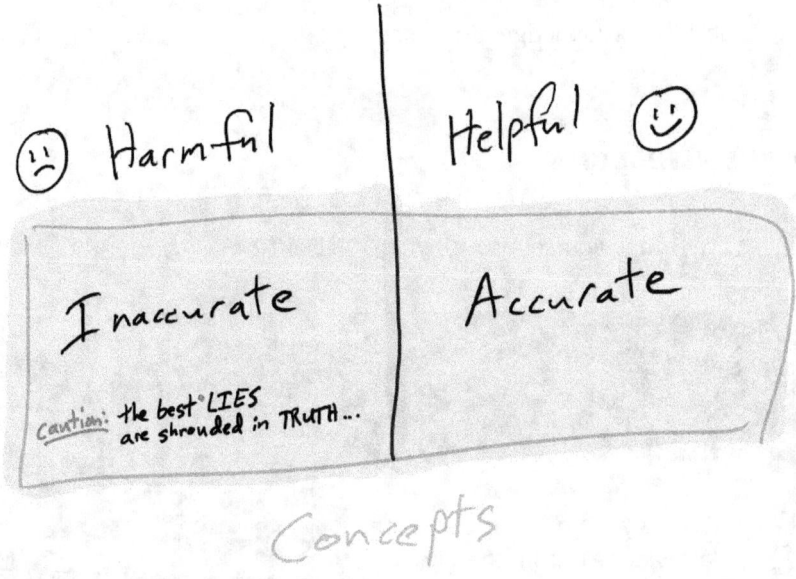

😟 Harmful | Helpful 🙂

Inaccurate | Accurate

Caution: the best LIES are shrouded in TRUTH...

Concepts

The concepts and mindsets which are accurate will serve you well.

When you act on inaccurate knowledge, you'll expect one thing, and get another.

Let's pretend you have the inaccurate beliefs:

- Calories don't count
- Healthy = good for weight loss

So you snack on "healthy nuts" ad libitum (as much as you want) thinking it's great for weight loss.

After gaining 10lbs, you're stuck scratching your head...

- Accurate knowledge helps.

· Inaccurate knowledge hinders.

2. KNOWLEDGE GAPS

These are things you're AWARE you DON'T KNOW

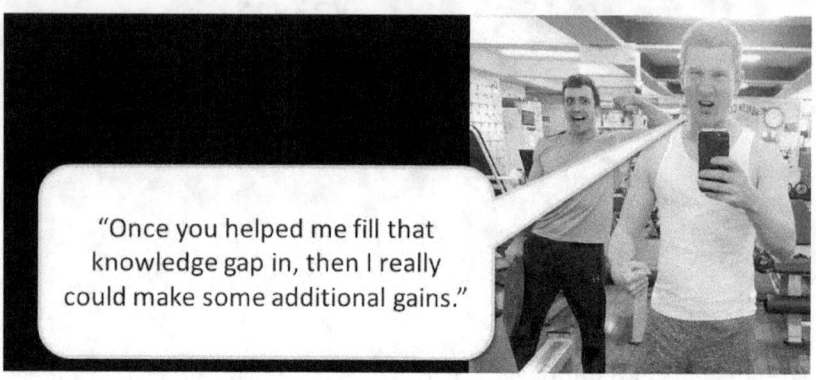

"Once you helped me fill that knowledge gap in, then I really could make some additional gains."

These are burning questions you've been waiting to ask an expert...

· Are eggs "bad" for me?
· Should I do crunches to get abs?
· What supplements should I take?
· How much cardio do I need to do?
· Is red meat dangerous?

There's an infinite list of questions.

And I never know what's going to come out of left field...

But most of the time my job is:

- Putting needless fears to rest
- Sharing knowledge
- Troubleshooting

And steering clients away from majoring in the minors, or shiny object syndrome.

Knowledge gaps are frustrating.

But with a trusted coach in your corner, getting answers is easy.

As the story goes, you don't pay a mechanic $200 for a 2 minute fix. You pay him $200 for fixing something in 2 minutes that would take you hours, days or MONTHS to fix on your own.

The same goes for coaching.

Only about half of dieters need a coach to get lean for life. The other half can do it on their own.

But does it make sense?

If you want better results, faster, with less work — then coaching may be for you.

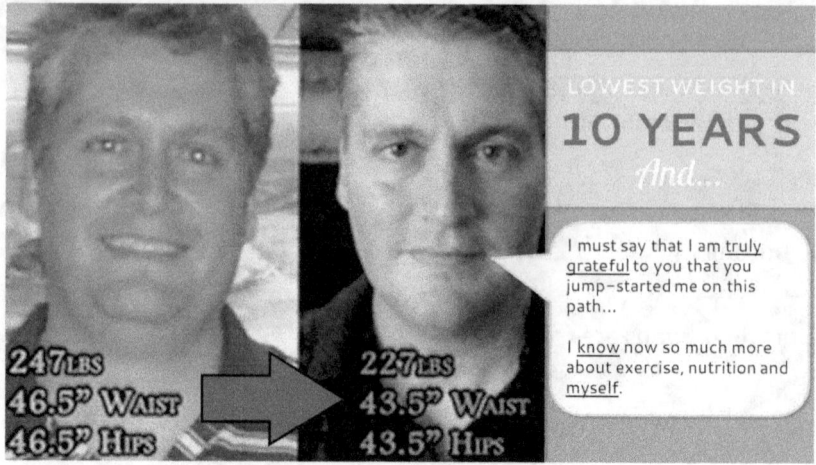

Eric is now at 210 lbs and still getting leaner...

3. HIDDEN STRENGTHS

These are the things you're UNAWARE you KNOW.

Many people don't know their strengths. And this is a weakness because those with high awareness are 9x more likely to flourish. They experience more:

- Happiness
- Energy
- Confidence
- Achievement

And better relationships.

As well as reductions in:

- Stress
- Depression

Weight loss becomes easier & more enjoyable when using your strengths. So if you don't know what they are, or how to use them...

Don't worry.

I've got you covered.

To identify your strengths & start using them, check out the bonuses at:

www.LeanForLifeBook.com/Bonus/

4. BLIND SPOTS

We all have things we're UNAWARE we DON'T KNOW.

Like Adam, you don't "know it" till you "show it."

When we uncover blind spots, it's like striking gold.

THIS is why you're struggling!

When we shed light on your blind spots, weight loss is a cinch. You feel like a weight has been lifted off your shoulders.

Take post-workout drinks for example.

This practice of:

- Doing a workout to burn extra fat
- Followed by a high-calorie smoothie...

Completely cancel each other out!

Luckily, all the nonsense in this industry makes my job easy...

- Stop the post-workout smoothie
- Eat when it's meal time

And voila!

You start losing weight again.

Your 4 blind spots are:

- Inaccurate knowledge
- Knowledge gaps
- Hidden strengths
- Things you don't know you don't know

And we bring them to light with the 4 T's:

- Training
- Tools
- Templates
- Troubleshooting

You'll get these with the blueprint & bonuses.

But first, you need the knowledge which informs the blueprint. Once your weight loss knowledge is accurate, you start getting the results you expect...

Everything becomes easier.

It starts with the fundamental concept in weight loss...

16

Knowledge: The Fundamental Concept

"It is difficult to speak of the universal specifically."
-Horace

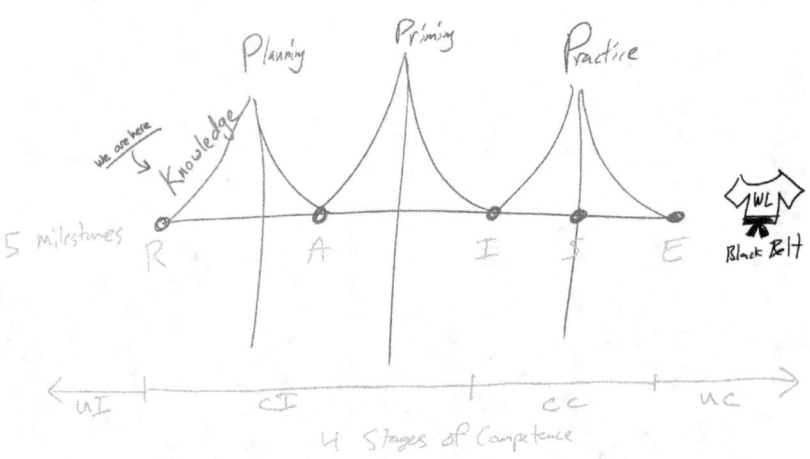

Your body is a complex system with inter-dependent parts. Because of this, weight loss at the MICRO level gets complicated FAST.

To see how, check out:

www.LeanForLifeBook.com/Complexity/

But how weight loss works at the MACRO level is EASY.

Here's the big picture:

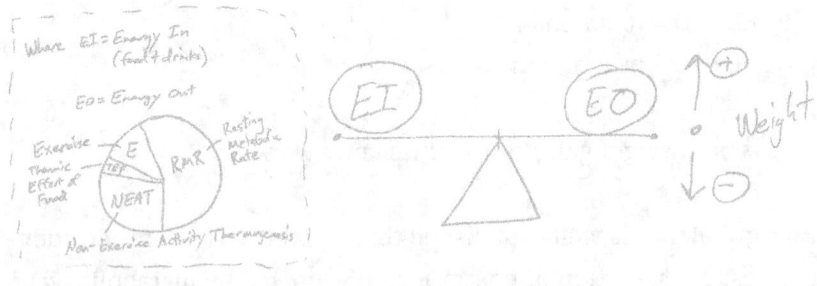

Energy In (EI)

Energy going into your body (eating, drinking, etc.).

Energy Out (EO)

Energy coming out out of your body (heat/matter [sweat, feces, etc.]).

RMR - Resting Metabolic Rate

Energy used in keeping you alive (thinking, breathing, pumping your heart, etc.).

Exercise

Energy used for moderate-high intensity movement.

NEAT - Non-Exercise Activity Thermogenesis

Energy used for low-intensity movement.

TEF – Thermic Effect of Food
Energy used for digestion.

Over time, you'll see one of 3 trends:

1. EI > EO → weight gain
2. EI = EO → maintenance
3. EI < EO → weight loss

This is how weight gain/loss/maintenance works.

Energy balance is well established through the 1st law of thermody-namics (conservation of energy). And validated by metabolic ward studies.

But some people disagree.

These people are:

· Dietary predators (taking advantage of your ignorance)
· Misinformed (sharing inaccurate knowledge unintentionally)
· Delusional (wanting reality to be different than it is)

And because of all this misinformation, the truth gets lost in the noise.

"In god we trust, all others must bring data."
–W. Edwards Deming

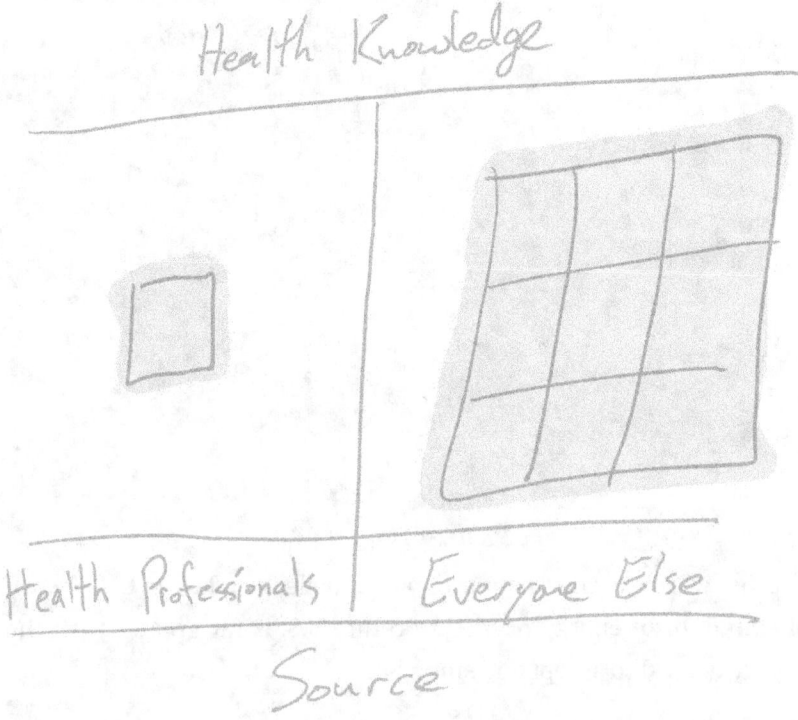

Misinformation is like a weed...

Once it takes root, it spreads & becomes hard to remove. Alberto Brandolini calls this the, **"Bullshit Asymmetry Principle."** He says, "The amount of energy needed to refute bullshit is an order of magnitude bigger than to produce it."

Visually, it looks like this:

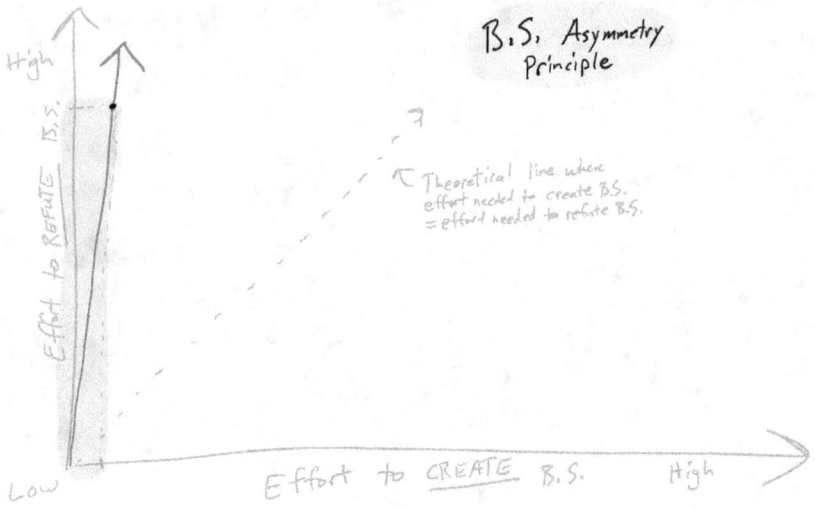

In other words, correcting inaccurate knowledge takes a TON of work. The amount of energy needed to refute B.S. is far greater than the energy needed to accept and spread it.

This is why some myths will never die.

For example, such "reasonable-sounding" statements such as:

- "Fat makes you fat"
- "Healthy foods are good for weight loss"
- "Hydroxylic acid, a compound used in Hitler's death camps, is poisoning your food"

May seem innocent enough at first glance... and bypass your baloney detector.

But they take time, attention, education and humility to correct. And if left uncorrected, these beliefs may waste years of time, money & effort.

Taken to extremes, believers:

- Miss-out on essential nutrients
- Fail to lose weight while eating "healthy"
- Start worrying about imaginary threats

For example, the hydroxylic acid used in Hitler's death camps...

It's the inorganic chemistry name for _water._

There's an entire brand of health/weight loss based on removing "toxins." And after reviewing 100s of these claims, I have yet to find ONE which isn't B.S.

Paracelsus said, "the dose makes the poison."

This is as true of water as anything else.

Just because something CAN be bad for you, doesn't mean it's a "toxin..."

The point is:

- B.S. is everywhere
- It takes time & effort to correct
- Especially when people don't like being wrong
- Or looking like fools

And according to the U.S. Department of Health & Human Services...

Only 12% of U.S. adults have proficient health literacy.

To protect yourself from misinformation, I recommend the skeptic links founds in the book bonuses at:

www.LeanForLifeBook.com/Bonus/

And after hearing a claim, mentally add, "In mice from another dimension, where 666% of statistics are made up on the spot."

For example, "Milk is toxic," becomes, "Milk is toxic in mice from another dimension where 666% of statistics are made up on the spot."

Can milk cause digestive issues?

Definitely.

Are some people lactose intolerant?

You bet.

Does that make milk toxic?

Hell no.

Philip Dormer Stanhope says, "Let blockheads read what blockheads wrote."

ALL claims (especially health claims) deserve a <u>healthy dose of skepticism.</u>

99% of the weight loss blogs, books & discussions aren't worth your time. So don't read them thinking they'll improve your life or results.

If you stumble on something important, you can always go to the source of the claim. Read it, discuss it, and do your best to determine if it's valid, invalid or inconclusive.

Then, if you decide to share the findings, you'll be in a much better position to:

- Explain your rationale
- Not look like a fool

As for the fundamental concept...

Make EI < EO.

Do this, and you lose weight.

Period.

A common mistake is to interpret this as...

"Eat Less, Exercise More."

Which is not as accurate as "Make EI < EO."

So people have problems when they:

- Just cut calories (hunger)
- Just increase activity (not addressing EI)
- Cut calories & increase activity (hungry & tired)

And miss solutions like:

- "Eat More, Exercise More" (my favorite)
- "Eat Less, Exercise Less"

These approaches produce the strongest & leanest physiques on the planet...

Olympic sprinters, swimmers, etc. often eat more & exercise more.

And they get RIPPED to shreds.

Likewise, professional bodybuilders often eat less & exercise less before a competition. And for a day or two, they have the leanest physiques on the planet.

"Eat less, exercise more" doesn't GUARANTEE weight loss.

But EI < EO does.

Here's how to make it happen...

17

Knowledge: S.T.A.N.D. Up

If you're OVER-weight, you're UNDER-S.T.A.N.D.ing.

There are 5 skills I have every client master before doing anything fancy.

We call it "S.T.A.N.D.ing up."

S.T.A.N.D. is an acronym for:

- (S)leep
- (T)raining
- (A)wareness
- (N)EPA (non-exercise physical activity)
- (D)iet

Alone, each of these skills tip the energy balance scales in your favor. Each makes it easier to get lean, and harder to gain fat.

Together, they're synergistic. Amplifying the effects of one another.

S.T.A.N.D.ing up is the FOUNDATION of getting lean for life...

Fail to build a strong foundation, and your results will be unimpressive and fleeting.

Build a solid foundation, and it will serve you well for a lifetime.

Here's how it works...

18

The "S" in S.T.A.N.D.ing Up

"Sleep is the golden chain that ties health and our bodies together."
–Thomas Dekker

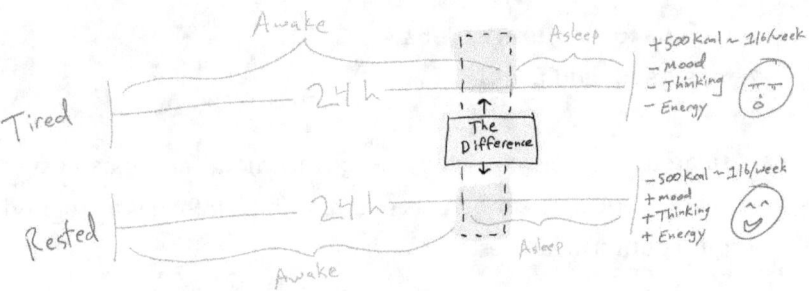

People who **(S)leep** less, eat more.

Sleep helps because those who sleep more:

- Eat less (enough to lose ~1 pound of fat weekly)
- Experience less stress

- Tend to make better choices
- Have more energy, willpower & better mood

As a result:

- You look better
- You feel better
- And you're more fun to be around

Being a sleep deprived zombie is no way to live...

And it's terrible for weight loss.

Been there, done that.

The national sleep foundation recommends:

- 7-9 hours for adults age 18-64
- 7-8 hours for adults 65+

Sleep related crashes cost the US government and businesses ~$46,000,000,000 per year... and is so important, NASA has a program for fatigue countermeasures.

A simple nap can DOUBLE alertness. And improve performance by as much as 30 percent.

So whether you're looking to look, feel or perform better...

Get your ZZZ's.

19

The "T" in S.T.A.N.D.ing Up

*"Things which matter most must never be at the mercy
of things which matter least."*
—Johann Wolfgang von Gothe

Contrary to popular belief, **(T)raining** itself doesn't burn many calories. It's almost always easier to lose weight by eating less rather than exercising more.

Look at the diagram again:

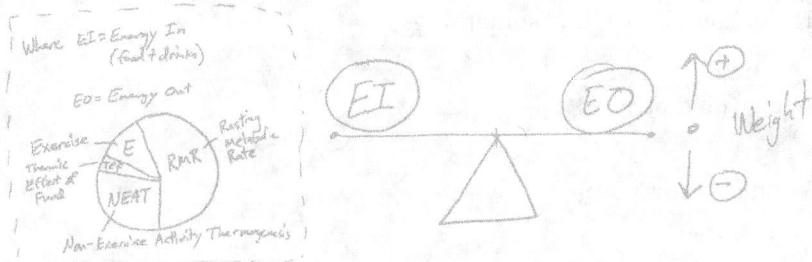

And notice how small the "E" is compared to the rest of the pie.

We'll define training as "high intensity exercise."

This means:

- Heavy breathing
- Hard or impossible to talk
- High muscle / nervous system fatigue

What type of training should you do?

The kind which:

- Your body can handle it (doctor approved)
- You LOVE doing

I love weight training.

My brother loves rock climbing. Others love boxing, rowing, etc.

What do you love?

If you don't know, find something.

And go do that.

Training helps you:

- Increase EO (calorie burn)
- Send less EI to fat

- And more to muscle

Most people think about EO, but miss the most important benefit...

BETTER NUTRIENT PARTITIONING.

Consistent training creates better nutrient partitioning. Where your body sends more nutrients to muscle, and fewer to fat.

This helps you:

- Look better
- By "targeting fat"
- And building/sparing muscle

In general:

- Fat looks bad
- Muscle looks good

When someone tells me their weight over the phone, I have no idea how they look...

Because weight doesn't determine your looks.

BODY COMPOSITION does.

Your body composition is how much fat you carry relative to muscle.

Less fat & more muscle = better body composition.

To see why, consider a 200lb man.

If he is 40% bodyfat, he has:

- 80lbs of fat
- 120lbs of lean body mass (LBM = muscle, bones, etc.)

No matter what your scale weight is, 40% bodyfat doesn't look good.

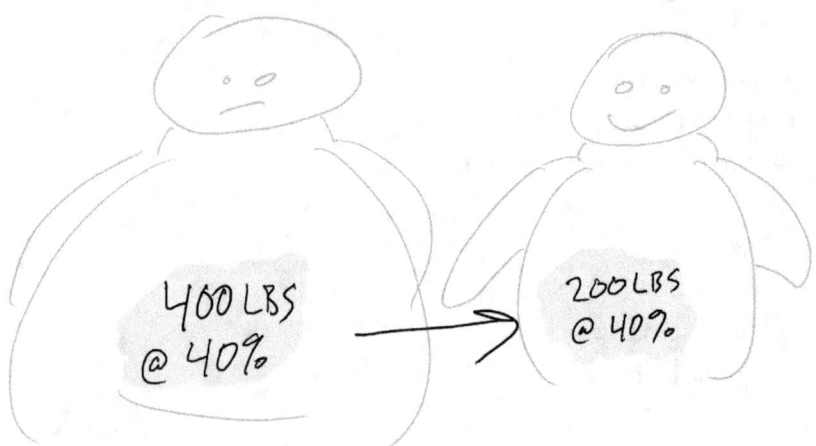

If you go from 400lbs @ 40% to 200lbs @ 40% you'll:

- Be smaller
- Be healthier
- Feel better

But you'll still LOOK FAT because you haven't improved your body composition.

When you get small enough, you look **"skinny-fat."**

We'll discuss skinny-fat problems more in a minute...

If our 200lb guy is 10% bodyfat, he has:

- 20lbs of fat
- 180lbs of LBM

At 10% bodyfat, most guys have a nice set of abs.

The important point is this:

Weight loss doesn't make you look better 100% of the time...

But FAT LOSS does.

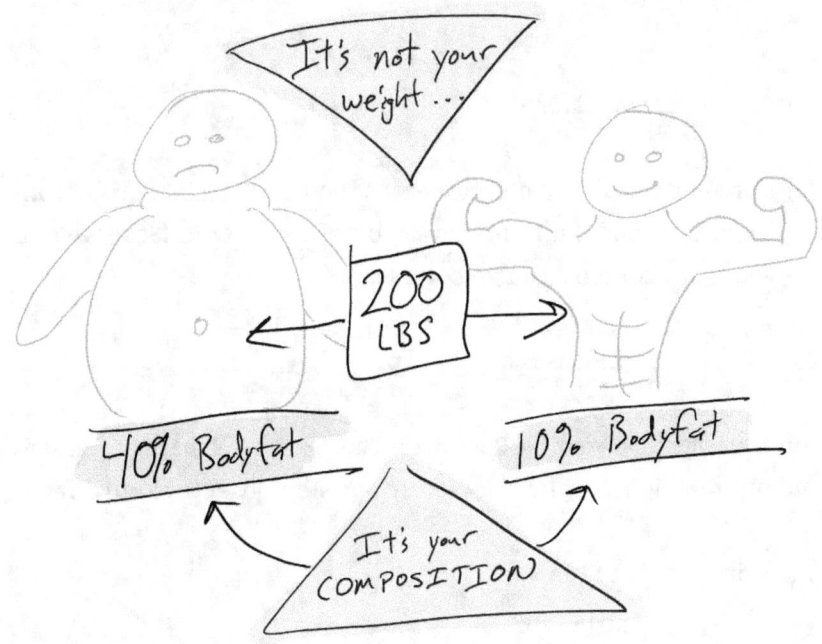

Pretend you create a 500kcal energy deficit per day for 1 week. And you lose 5lbs...

- Are you happy?
- SHOULD you be?

It depends on where the weight loss came from.

By creating a 3,500kcal deficit, you could lose:

- 1lb of fat (~3,500kcal/lb)
- 5lbs of muscle (~700kcal/lb * 5lbs)
- Fat & muscle (1-5lbs from the same ~3,500 kcal)

When you lose 5lbs, it's hard to know where the weight loss comes from.

Is it fat, muscle or water?

Let's pretend it's 5lbs of muscle because you don't train. You go from 200lbs @ 20% bodyfat to 195lbs @ 20.5% bodyfat. You lose weight, but your body composition gets worse.

Your 5lbs of weight loss is a total flop.

You're weaker and your BMR is lower. This makes weight regain easier, and future weight loss harder. You're one step closer to skinny-fat...

And skinny fat isn't fun.

Especially if you're a guy. This is where you have man boobs instead of a rock-hard chest. Love handles instead of abs. Bulky arms instead of bulging biceps.

And ladies look "flabby" or "flat" instead of "toned."

They're smaller, but still have flabby arms, saggy butts and a jiggle-belly.

To avoid these fates, you need to train.

- Training improves nutrient partitioning
- Better nutrient partitioning improves body composition
- And better body composition makes you look better...

REGARDLESS of the weight on the scale.

Here's a talk I've had with many clients...
"Nick, I'm not losing any weight!"
"But are you losing inches around your waist?"
"Well... yes."
"So what's the problem?"

When you first start training, the scale weight might not move (because you're adding muscle). But if your weight stays the same, that's a good thing. It means you're losing fat & gaining muscle.

Fat loss & muscle gain are just cancelling each other out on the scale.

This is why you look better at the same weight.

Pretend you start training at 20% bodyfat @ 200lbs. And you become

15% bodyfat at 200lbs.

The results it:

- 10lbs less fat
- 10lbs more muscle

You're still the same weight, but you look better.

"But Nick, I don't want to gain muscle because of __(reason)__."

This is a novice concern.

You'll NEVER hear it from a master because it's a needless fear.

ESPECIALLY for the ladies.

So let's clear it up.

Ladies...

Training won't turn you into a bald female bodybuilder with a mustache. Pro female bodybuilders look like this because they inject themselves with male hormones...

But you have 1/100th the testosterone of a man. And alpha males with 200x more testosterone than you still struggle to gain muscle.

So don't worry about getting "too big."

It won't happen.

What might happen is you gain muscle faster than losing fat. This only lasts a short while. So give it time.

Once fat loss starts outpacing your muscle gain, you'll look like a sexy Goddess. You'll have tight arms, a tight ass...

You'll be TIGHT!

This "toned" or "ripped" look you're going for is "skin on muscle."

- Not skin on fat
- Not skin on bone

Skin on muscle.

So obsess less about the number on the scale, and more about consistency with training. Because whether you're gaining, maintaining or losing weight, training makes you look better.

While losing weight with consistent training, you:

- Lose less muscle
- And more fat

While maintaining weight with consistent training, you:

- Send more nutrients to muscle
- And fewer to fat

While gaining weight with consistent training, you:

- Send more nutrients to muscle
- And fewer to fat

Regardless of what's happening on the scale...

Training makes you look better.

Now, you can't outrun a bad diet...

But whatever your diet may be, training helps.

20

The "A" in S.T.A.N.D.ing Up

"An enormous portion of cognitive activity is non-conscious, figuratively speaking, it could be 99 percent; we probably will never know precisely how much is outside awareness."
-Dr. Emmanuel Donchin

Increasing **(A)wareness** gives you 2 super powers:

1. More options
2. Better choices

1. More options

Having more good options makes a world of difference.

For example, let's pretend you learn, "Dieters who log their food lose, on average, TWICE as much weight as those who don't."

So now, when it's mealtime, you have a choice:

- Log your food
- Or don't

Even if you decide NOT to log your food 99% of the time...

A 1% improvement is still an improvement.

It counts.

And going from 0% improvement (no awareness) to 1% improvement (because you now have a choice) is HUGE!

- 1% turns into 5%...
- 5% becomes 10%...
- 10% becomes 20%...

Before you know it:

- You're logging your food
- Your awareness is higher than ever
- You start seeing WHY you're overweight

And making better choices...

2. Making Better choices

As you pay attention to things you didn't focus on before, you learn more.

You realize your food choices impact your:

- Weight
- Mood
- Thinking
- Alertness

And more.

You increase the accuracy of your worldview. You pay more attention to the impact of your choices. And this makes it easier to make the right ones.

Let's pretend you start logging your food to increase awareness.

If you're like me, you LOVE beer and LIKE Oreos.

Seriously, who doesn't like Oreos?!

But one day, you decide to look at the calories.

And your search reveals:

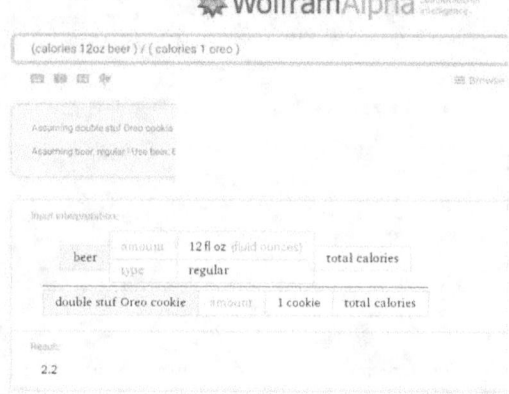

1 beer = 2.2 double stuffed Oreos

And you just ate a whole package...

You could have had a lot of good beer...

But instead, you opted for a little enjoyment, and a lot of guilt.

Personally, I'd rather have 15 beers.

EVERY time.

No exceptions.

Because you need to CHOOSE your battles.

When I go to the store, I CHOOSE not to put Oreos in my shopping cart. Not because I don't like them (I do), but because I like other things more.

In fact, I CHOOSE not to walk down the Oreo aisle at all...

There are other aisles with foods I enjoy more. And snacks which are more nutritious, satiating and enjoyable with fewer calories.

But without awareness, you're in the dark. You can't see what's right in front of you.

You CAN'T improve, even if you want to...

21

The "N" in S.T.A.N.D.ing Up

"PLAY: Work you do for free."
-Steven Wright

Lean people move more.

Not because they HAVE to, but because they WANT to. They FEEL like moving more... naturally, without any special prodding.

The leaner you get, the more you will too.

But until then, you're going to have to work at it. Luckily, it's not really "work." Regular **(N)EPA** (non-exercise physical activity) breaks have many benefits. These breaks:

- Decrease hunger (lowering EI)
- Burn extra calories (increasing EO)
- Improve mood & circulation

They're fun, rejuvenating & good for weight loss.

After an hour of writing, I take a short NEPA break to enjoy:

- "Sun time" outside
- Juggling
- Walking
- Stretching
- Etc.

A smart watch will even tell you "it's time to move." So if you're looking for an easy way to remember, a smart watch can help.

Next time you find yourself sitting on your butt for too long...

Freshen up with a bit of NEPA.

Your body, mind & waistline will thank you.

22

The "D" in S.T.A.N.D.ing Up

"Eat food. Not too much. Mostly plants."
–Michael Pollan

A better **(D)iet** will help you feel more full on fewer calories.

Here's the template I give my clients. You can use it to increase the volume, satiety and nutrient density of your meals.

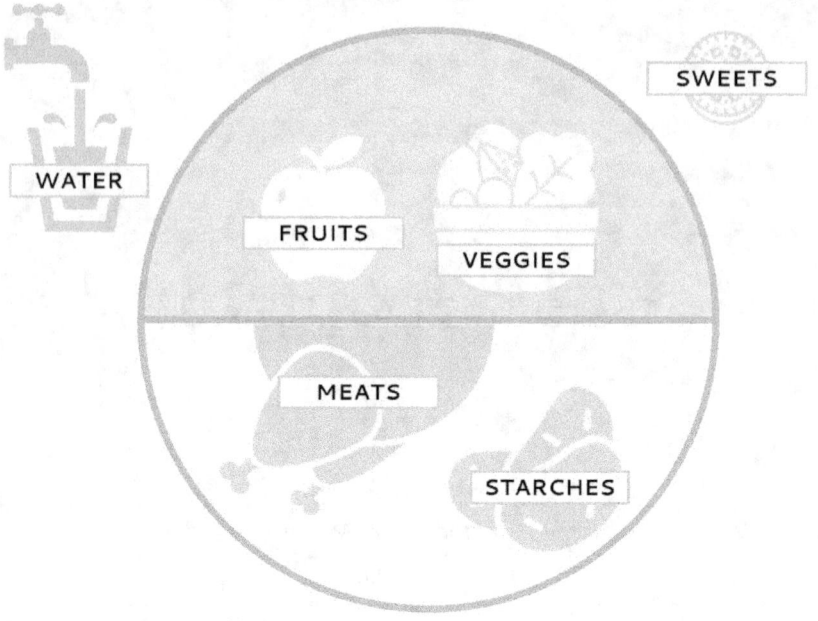

It's similar to the Harvard "Healthy Eating Plate." With a few key differences:

- No emphasis on whole grains
- No split between fruits and veg
- No inclusion of healthy fats

This template gives you more flexibility, and less woo.

Whole grains are harmful/helpful depending on individual circumstances. They're not "universally better" than other carbohydrate sources.

The total volume of fruit/veg is more important than an even distribution.

And when following the template, most clients get plenty of fat. Sources include:

- Meat
- Junk food
- Oils used in cooking/salads
- Nuts/avocados/etc.

Your goal is to:

- Eat fresh, real food
- Drink mostly water (or no/low-calorie like coffee/tea)
- Observe "hara hachi bun me" (eat to 80% fullness)
- Aim for the prescribed portions (fruit + veg = everything else)

Sweets are optional.

In my travels through Asia and Europe, I learned much of the world considers fresh fruit a perfectly fine dessert.

The cookie is there to remind you that if you have sweets...

Have a taste, not a tin.

The first 3 bites of anything are the best. When you're eating sugar-frosted sugar cake drowned in sugar syrup... more than a few bites is overkill.

For the most part, WHAT to eat isn't complicated.

When it is, you need to be talking to a qualified medical professional.

NOT rolling the dice on a potential life-or-death issue.

But most people are "OK" with WHAT to eat...

We're omnivores. We can thrive on plants AND animals.

There's TONS of flexibility.

Maybe too much...

That's why "WHAT" to eat isn't as tricky as "HOW" to eat for fat loss.

This is where the above template, and your weight loss blueprint, come in handy...

23

S.T.A.N.D. Up Summary

*"True enjoyment comes from activity of the mind
and exercise of the body; the two are ever united."*
–Wilhelm Von Humboldt

Here's a recap of how S.T.A.N.D.ing up tips scales in your favor:

	EI	EO	Results
S	Less Eating @Night ↓EI (~500 kcal/day)	↑Recovery	• Lose 1lb/week (7x 500kcal) • Look better • Feel better
T	X	↑EO ↑Partitioning	• More fat loss • Less muscle loss
A	Better Choices ↓EI	More Opportunities ↑EO	• 2x total weight loss (with food logging alone) • More & better choices (∞ impact)
N	Lowers Appetite ↓EI	More Movement ↑EO	• More Energy • More Alert • Easier to get & stay lean
D	↑Enjoyment satiety Nutrients ↓EI	Increase TEF ↑EO	• Look better • Eat more (volume) • Easier weight loss

Alone, each of these help.

But together, they have <u>synergistic</u> effects.

For example, more sleep may help you be more alert (awareness). More awareness helps you make better choices. You have more energy for NEPA & training. Your diet improves. The nutrient partitioning from your training amplifies all of the above.

In short, you look and feel better...

Easier than ever.

For more on "What successful dieters do differently..."

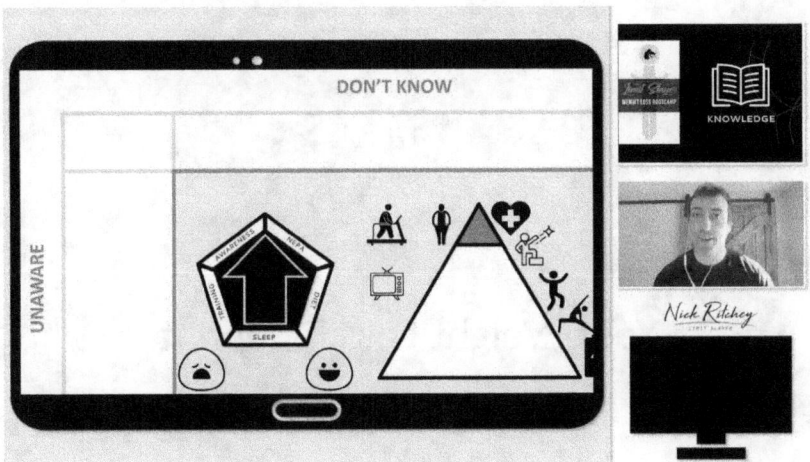

Check out your free bonuses at:

www.LeanForLifeBook.com/Bonus/

Improving your S.T.A.N.D.ing gets you 80% of the way to BlackBelt.

Now that you know WHAT to do, let's make it happen!

24

Your Weight Loss Blueprint

"Success is nothing more
than a few simple disciplines,
practiced every day."
–Jim Rohn

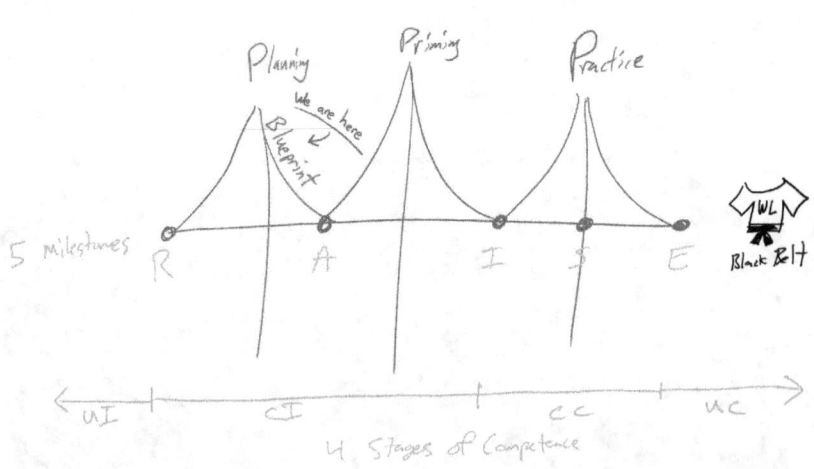

Pretend you're lost & alone.

And you want to get home ASAP.

Do you...

1. Open your GPS to find where you are?
2. Or start walking in a random direction?

Most dieters are so anxious to get started, they choose #2. And head off in a random direction. Only becoming more lost...

Don't be like them.

To give you directions, your GPS needs 2 things:

1. Where you are (your current S.T.A.N.D.ing)
2. Where you want to go (weight loss BlackBelt)

Let's find where you are in each of the 5 skills right now, so we can help you get to mastery as soon as possible.

We'll use a simple traffic light system.

The goal is to turn all lights GREEN.

Bootcamp goes into each traffic light in detail.

But let's keep it short & sweet, so you get a quick idea of:

- How you're doing
- What needs to improve
- And where to begin.

The traffic lights are:

- GREEN: you are consistent, and your skill is high
- YELLOW: there's room for improvement
- RED: you are inconsistent or your skill is low

How's your S.T.A.N.D.ing?

To find out, read the following.

And circle your color (Red / Yellow / Green) for each question.

SLEEP

- R / Y / G - Do you go to bed when tired?
- R / Y / G - Sleep well throughout the night?
- R / Y / G - And wake up fully refreshed in the morning WITHOUT an alarm?

TRAINING

- R / Y / G - Do you enjoy pain-free training?
- R / Y / G - With high intensity?
- R / Y / G - At least 3 times per week?

AWARENESS

- R / Y / G - Do you monitor your S.T.A.N.D.ing daily?
- R / Y / G - Capture recurring & painful problems?
- R / Y / G - And have a simple system for turning pain into power?

NEPA

Do you engage in:

- R / Y / G - At least 30 minutes of daily...
- R / Y / G - Pain-free...
- R / Y / G - Moderate-high intensity activity?

DIET

Does the majority of your diet consist of:

- R / Y / G - High-satiety (filling)...
- R / Y / G - Nutrient-dense (nutritious)...
- R / Y / G - Calorie-sparse (low-calorie)...
- R / Y / G - Real (unprocessed) food...
- R / Y / G - Which you love to eat?

After looking at the details, we zoom back out. And rate your global S.T.A.N.D.ing for each of the 5 skills. Where:

- RED: No green lights
- YELLOW: Some green lights
- GREEN: All green lights

So if you have all greens in sleep, sleep is GREEN. If you have some greens in training (but not all) you're training is YELLOW. If you have ZERO greens in awareness, your awareness is RED. Etc.

Getting to all green is like reaching Everest base camp.

You stop here BEFORE climbing to the top of the mountain (such as a bodybuilding competition). And you return here AFTER reaching the top (because stage-lean isn't sustainable).

These are the habits which make & keep you lean.

When all lights are green, we call this **"weight loss baseline."**

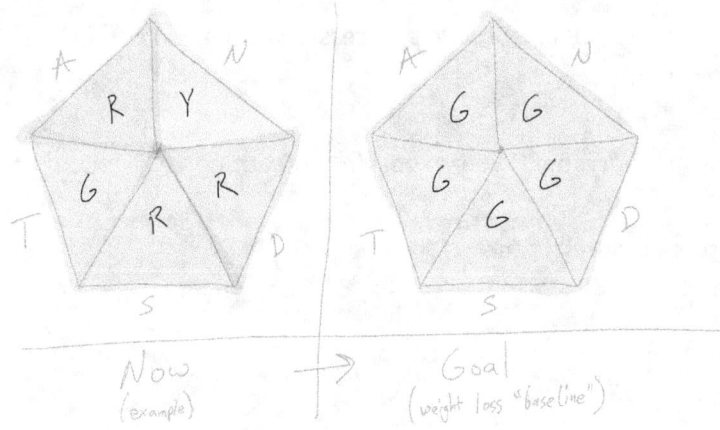

Imagine how much EASIER it will be to stay lean once you reach baseline...

- You're well rested in a pain-free, powerful body.
- Your diet is full of nutritious food you love to eat.
- Your confidence & energy are through the roof.
- You move more & better.

And your understanding of how weight loss works is crystal clear.

"S.T.A.N.D.ing Up" gets you to baseline.

And the progression is simple:

1. Choose 1 skill to focus on
2. Turn red into yellow
3. And yellow into green
4. Repeat until all lights are green.

This is the S.A.F.E. & Simple progression which makes you look & feel better than ever.

Easy in theory, but if you're missing something, it's hard in practice.

Here's the special sauce...

25

Blueprint: Grow with the Flow

"I walk slowly, but I never walk backwards."
-Abraham Lincoln

You've experienced it before.

It's the state:

- NBA players achieve when they're "on fire."
- You feel when you're "in the zone."

It's the state of optimal performance.

A state known as **"FLOW."**

And it's going to help you get leaner than ever...

Easier than ever.

I first learned about flow during my graduate studies in Applied

Positive Psychology at UPENN. Directly from its founder, Mihaly Csikszentmihalyi.

Since then, it's changed the way I approach EVERYTHING...

From cooking, to training, math lessons and book writing. It's one of the most powerful & practical tools in my toolbox.

Now YOU get to discover its power...

And flow all the way to weight loss BlackBelt...

Here's how it works:

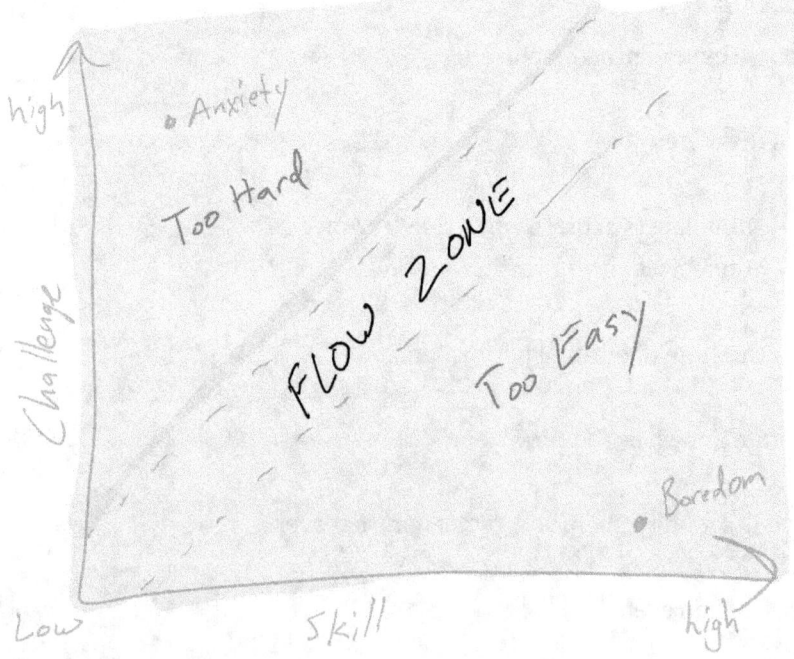

You "get into flow" when your skills are well matched to your challenges.

We call this the "flow zone."

It's where you have focus, work your best, and your sense of time disappears. Outside the flow zone, you struggle or feel bored. Because of too much/little challenge.

New gym-goers struggle because:

- Their skills are too low
- Their challenges are too high

This produces anxiety and requires heaps of motivation to overcome.

On the flip side of the coin, what's the #1 complaint of most gym rats who've been at it for a while?

"My workouts are so BORING!"

Boredom sets in when your skills improve, but your challenges don't.

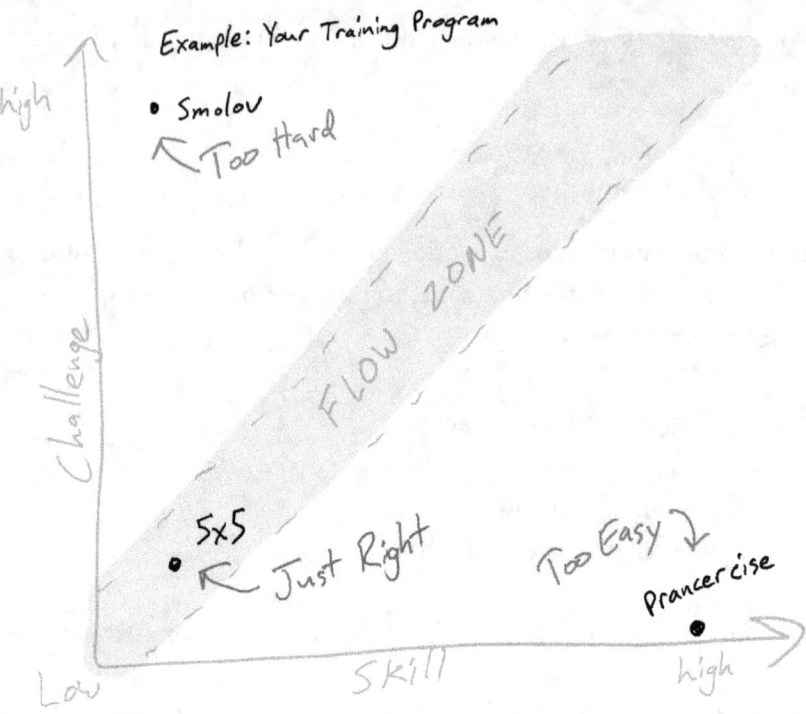

The key to making training enjoyable for life is to:

- Find something you love
- Which can challenge you for a lifetime
- And optimize for flow

In the beginning of any new skill acquisition, you usually need to DECREASE the challenge. Because you OVERESTIMATE your abilities.

Recall the Dunning-Kruger effect:

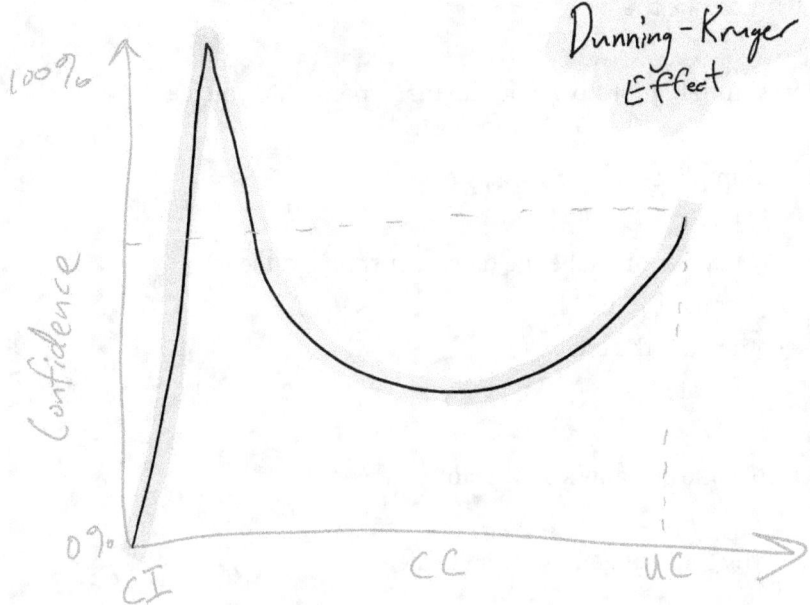

After New Year's Eve, you see this in spades when throngs of people swarm gyms worldwide...

They:

- Experience the Dunning–Kruger effect
- Try to do too much, too soon
- Get overwhelmed
- And give up

All because of a simple mismatch of skills vs. challenges.

They *could* and *should* decrease the challenge. But for various reasons (ego, limiting beliefs, declining motivation, etc.), they don't.

119

Don't be like them.

By optimizing for flow, you can master any skill you desire.

It's a simple 4-step process:

1. Match your challenge to your current skill level
2. Increase your skill
3. Increase the challenge
4. Repeat

Video game designers do this for you.

It's why the best games are so addictive.

They start you off at level 1. It's easy, but not boring. Then silently, in the background, they jack up the difficulty. Little by little. Bit by bit.

You feel challenged, but not too much.

You die, improve, and progress.

It's fun.

You're sucked into the game. And time disappears.

You're in flow.

Before you know it, you beat the final boss. You either quit the game because there's no new challenge...

Or continue with a "New Game +" mode, and greater difficulty.

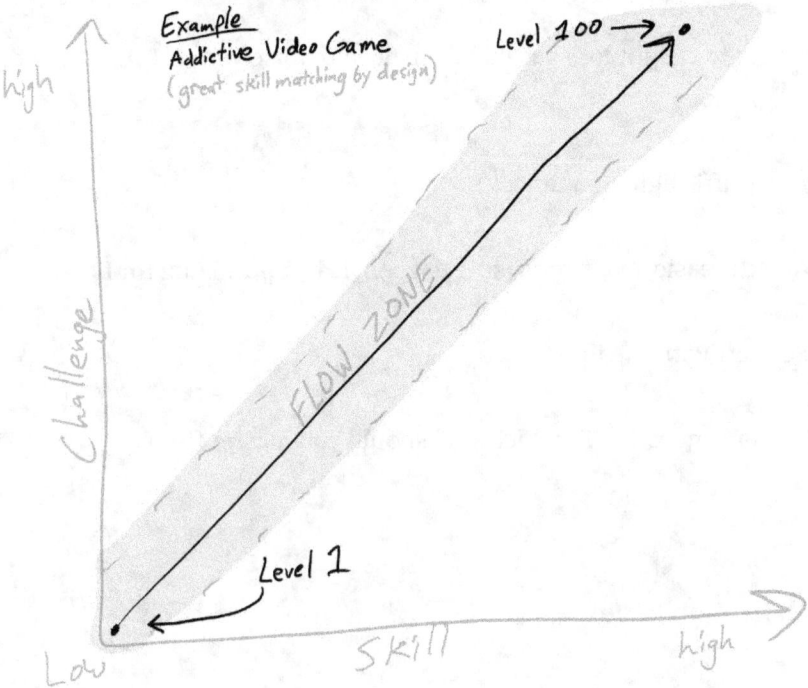

The game was never "that hard," but your skills end up on a completely different level from where you started.

As the Tanzanian proverb goes, "little by little, a little becomes a lot."

And most importantly, you have FUN in the process.

- Overwhelm is a sign of too much challenge
- Boredom is a sign of too little challenge

So next time you're feeling overwhelmed, recognize it as a signal to

MAKE THINGS EASIER on yourself. And the next time you're feeling bored, instead of getting complacent, CHALLENGE yourself.

To get to weight loss baseline, you need to raise your S.T.A.N.D.ing to all greens.

One traffic light at a time.

And the easiest way to make it happen, is by optimizing for flow...

So grow with the flow.

The only question is, which skill should you master first?

26

Blueprint: Where to Begin

"Planning is bringing the future into the present
so that you can do something about it now."
–Alan Lakein

If you're thinking, "Wow, I have a lot of yellow & red in my S.T.A.N.D.ing...

Where do I start?"

You're in luck.

I've created a quiz to help you identify your "Weight Loss Limiter." This is the #1 thing holding you back right now. Remove your limiter, and everything becomes easier.

You'll find the quiz with the bonuses at:
   www.LeanForLifeBook.com/Bonus/

Don't continue to the next chapter until you've taken the quiz and found your limiter.

If you skip ahead WITHOUT taking the quiz, the next chapters will be far less impactful.

So do yourself a favor, and go take the quiz:
  www.LeanForLifeBook.com/Bonus/

Then move on to the next chapter.

We'll get you to greens in no time.

27

The 2nd Pillar: Priming

*"Make the best use of what is in your power,
and take the rest as it happens."*
–Epictetus

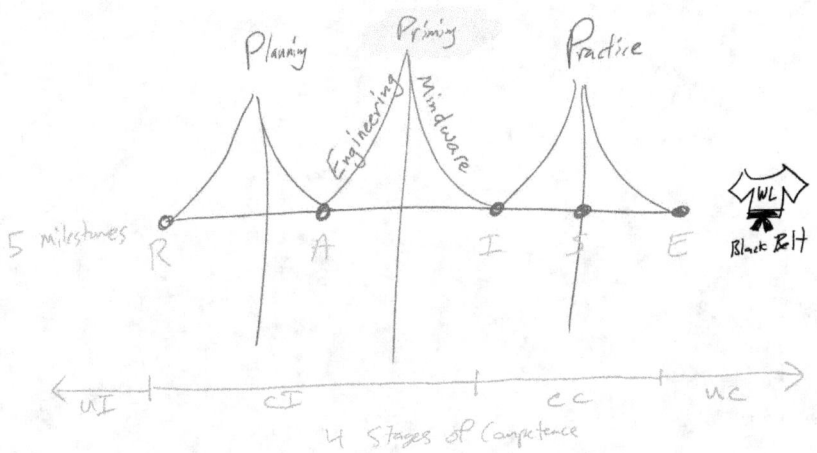

Things almost NEVER go perfectly according to plan.

But there are 2 things you can do to make it easier to stay on track...

28

Priming: Engineer for Success

"The things which are most important don't always scream the loudest."
–Bob Hawke

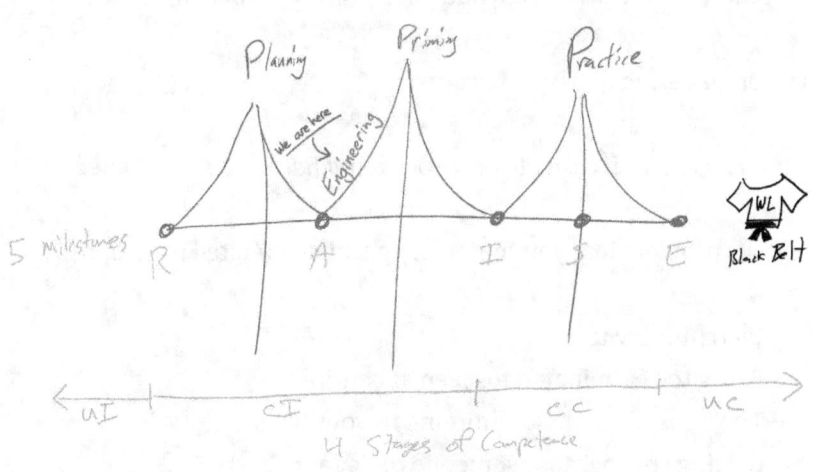

The key to engineering for success starts with a simple question.

"How can I make it easier to succeed, and harder to fail, in X?"

Where "X" is the Weight Loss Limiter you're focusing on improving. Let's call this, **"The Engineering Question."**

There are 5 keys to engineering amazing solutions:

1. Keeping a problem log (pain to power)
2. Activating B=MAT (practice)
3. Triggering A.L.E.R.T.S. (mindware)
4. Making it S.A.F.E. & Simple
5. Using feedback loops (mastery)

You haven't seen 4 of the keys yet, but we'll get to them soon. For now, here's an example to illustrate the power of good engineering.

Pretend your focus is sleep, and your problem is getting to bed.

The engineering question becomes:

"How can I make it easier to get to bed? And harder to stay up late?"

In your problem log, you find many problems related to sleep:

- Watching TV too late
- Being too caffeinated to sleep at bedtime
- Too many thoughts swimming in your head
- Getting cold because someone took your covers
- Waking up from noise

Let's pretend the biggest problem is: **"Watching TV too late."**

You ask yourself:

- "How can I make it easier to stop watching TV?
- And harder to start watching TV after bedtime?"

You look at each of the A.L.E.R.T.S. associated with your evening TV and notice Time + Location are consistent.

You use "Pain to Power" to come up with the following fix:

- Buy an outlet timer for $5 at Target
- Plug it into the outlet of your TV/modem/cable box
- Set it to turn off 30 minutes before bedtime

When your power goes off, it's time for bed.

This makes it easier to stop watching TV, because it's done for you. And harder to resume your show, because there isn't a quick fix.

To resume your show, you need to:

- Go to the outlet
- Change the settings
- Reboot everything
- Wait for it all to reboot
- Resume the show where you left off

And turn the outlet settings back to where they were before going to bed.

This $5 fix will help you:

- Eat less
- Sleep more
- Feel better every morning

And it...

- Requires ZERO willpower
- Makes it EASIER to make the right choice (going to bed)

By making it easy to succeed where it was nearly impossible before.

You do one final check to ensure your fix is S.A.F.E. & Simple.

It passes with flying colors.

So you go buy some outlet timers. Set them up, and start getting to bed earlier.

Before your know it, your sleep is GREEN.

You're rested, leaner and more energetic than ever.

Thanks to a 2-minute, $5 fix.

Compare this to binge watching Netflix BEFORE your outlet timer...

The thought of going to bed comes to mind.

Your show is on, and you're in the middle of the action.

How likely are you to pause your show, and go to bed?

For me, the answer is close to **ZERO.**

But if the TV turns itself off...

- AND you have time to think, "It's time for bed..."
- AND you have to stand up to change the timer...
- AND reboot everything
- AND wait for it all to start back up...
- And...

Screw it!

Might as well go to bed.

You can always pick up where you left off tomorrow. When everything is up and running. WITHOUT the hassle.

This is how a little engineering goes a long way.

When considering B=MAT, you've:

- Lowered the activation energy down to ZERO
- Increased your ability to turn off the TV to 100%
- AND created a trigger that works 100% of the time

So you'll have a 100% success rate in turning the TV off.

This doesn't mean you'll never resume your show...

But it does make it easier to get to bed on time.

And that's all we're going for.

Even if you turn everything back on 9 nights out of 10, it's still a 10% improvement from installing a $5 switch.

That's HUGE.

Imagine engineering similar fixes for ALL your weight loss limiters...

How easy would it be to get & stay lean?

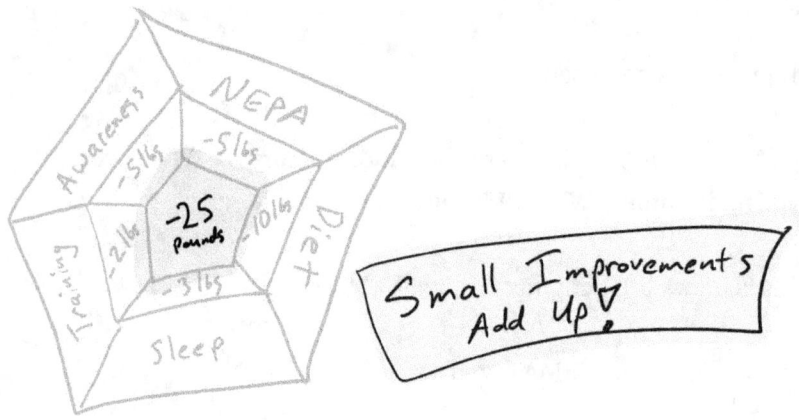

I love physical fixes, so I always look for them first.

But sometimes, there isn't a good physical fix. It's easier to change your mind than it is to change your environment. Other times, your physical fixes fail.

So you need a Plan B.

In both cases, you can make it easier to succeed and harder to fail...

With MINDWARE.

29

Priming: Master Your Mindware

"Until you make the unconscious conscious,
it will direct your life & you will call it fate."
–Carl Jung

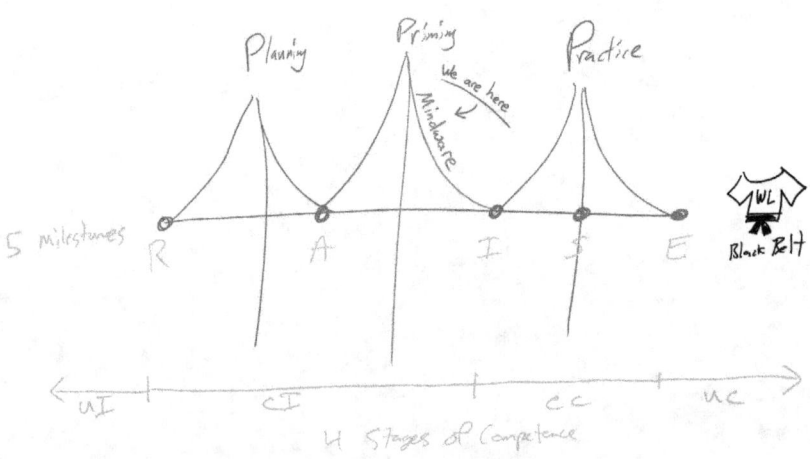

Ever eaten an entire bag of chips, jar of cookies, or tub of ice cream...

Without "DECIDING" to do so?

It happens.

But doesn't HAVE to.

Engineering your environments for success will help. If your weakness is ice cream, stop buying it at the store. If it's not in your house, you can't eat it when you're home alone.

Make a special trip to eat ice cream on special occasions.

Don't keep ticking time-bombs in your house...

Or your mind.

The Jung quote at the start of this chapter warns against the dangers of being a slave to your unconscious.

Hindsight is 20/20.

But few of us have such clarity when it matters.

We forget.

And repeat the same mistakes. Over & over. Even though we "know better." Because we forget what we know, when we need it the most.

This is where MINDWARE comes in.

Mindware (mind + software) is all about reprogramming your brain.

You can reprogram the way you think, feel and act with the right mindware.

It's how you engineer your brain for success.

So it's easier to make the right choices, and harder to make the wrong ones.

Of course, this assumes, you have a choice.

Freedom is optionality.

I create mindware to help my clients think the right things, at the right times, in the right ways... so they have OPTIONS where they had none before. These, in turn, give them the ability to CHOOSE better.

Less "fate," more freedom.

Having a choice, even if you only make a better choice 1% of the time, is better than failing 100% of the time.

In theory, this works. In practice, Oreos...

Let's pretend you've made your house a dietary safe haven. But one day, a friend comes over. And leaves a bag of Oreos on your table...

In the past, that bag would disappear into your belly before you even realized it. The (S)timulus would trigger an (U)nconscious (R)esponse, and the outcome is the entire bag in your belly.

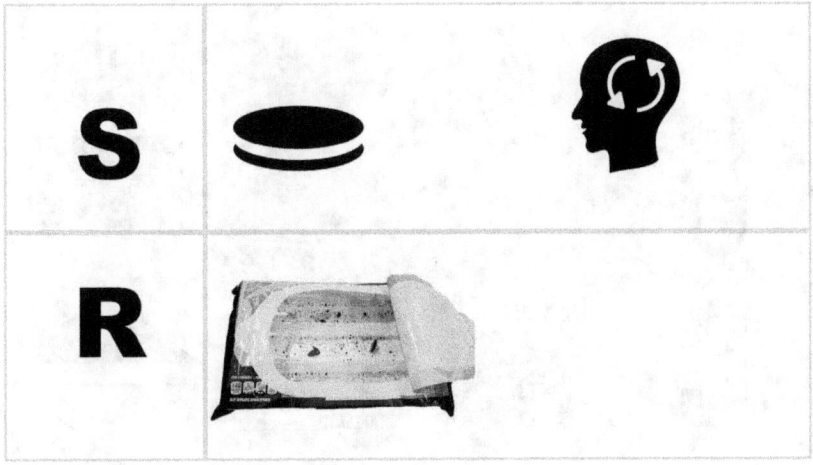

But now, with mindware, you:

- Make the (U)nsconsious, (C)onscious
- Put the brakes on sooner
- Mitigate the damage later

And experience better outcomes.

Here's an example of mindware you can create for yourself:

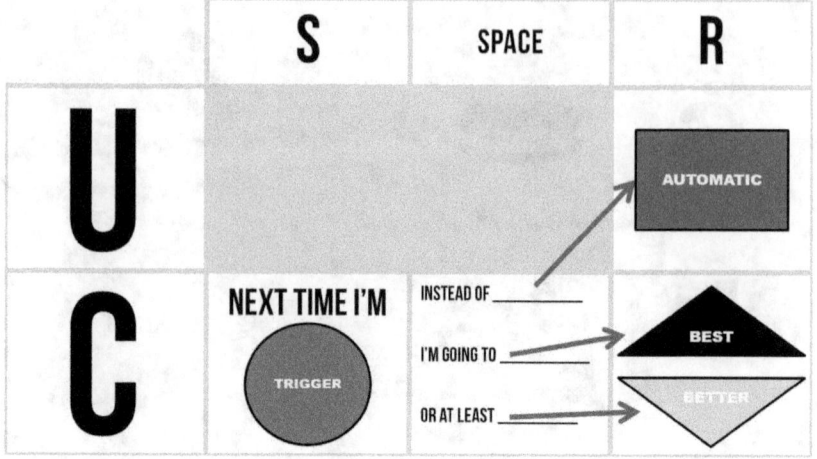

We'll cover triggers when we get to Milestone 4: Stagnation.

For now, let's assume you see the Oreos on the table & think:

- Instead of "eating the entire bag of Oreos"
- I'm going to "eat an apple"
- Or at least "not eat 3/4 of the bag"

Unlike the outlet timer, your mindware won't trigger 100% in the beginning.

But over time, it will trigger more & more.

Leading to better & better outcomes.

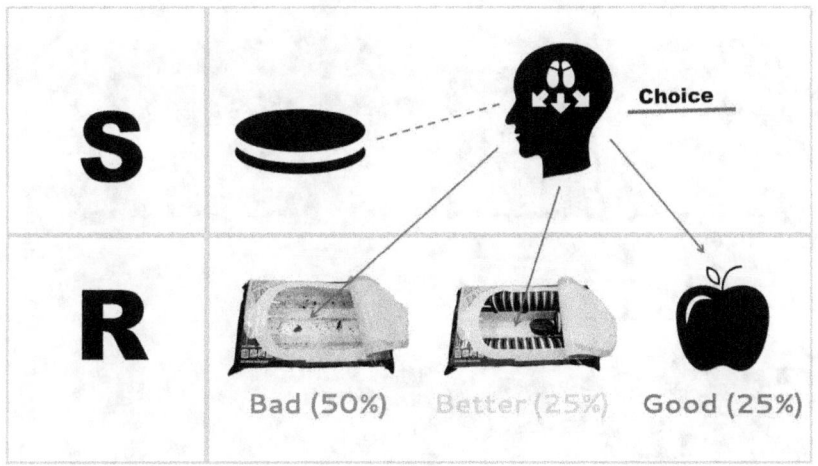

Even with imperfect mindware, you're better off.

Instead of eating the whole bag of Oreos 100% of the time, you may only eat it 50% of the time. 25% of the time you eat a quarter of the bag.

And 25% of the time you eat an apple instead.

You're still far from perfect, but this one choice alone may help you drop another 10-20lbs.

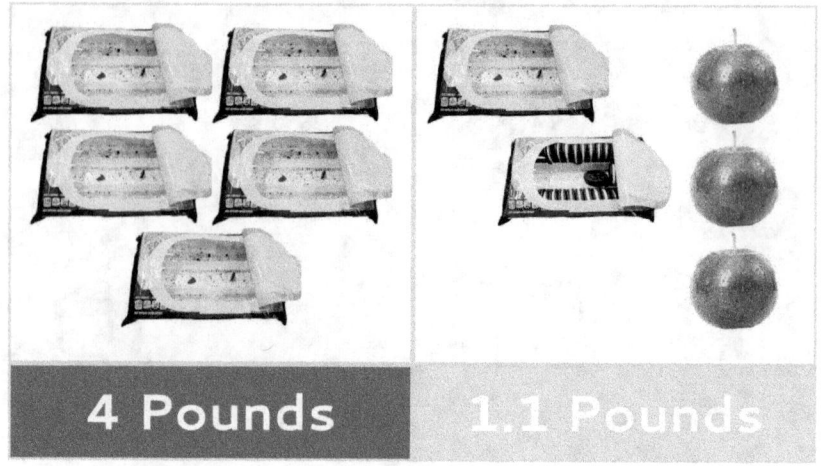

EVEN IF you're not 100% successful...

EVEN IF your mindware is imperfect...

ANY chance to improve is better than none.

What if you had even more opportunities to choose better?

In sleep, training, awareness, NEPA, diet, and beyond...

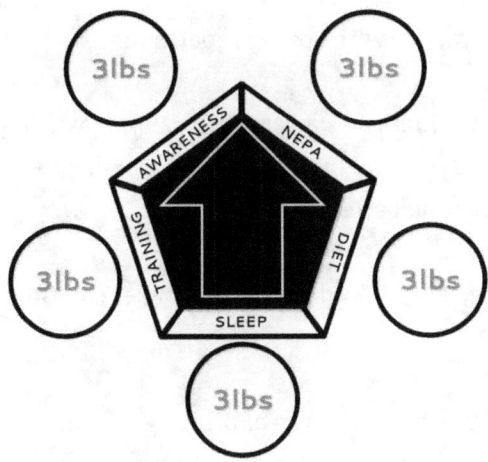

How much easier would it be to get & stay lean?

Creating mindware is an art.

It's easily the most powerful tool in my toolbox...

And deserves a book of its own.

Which is why I create mindware for my members, but don't teach them how to create their own... yet. It takes time and considerable skill to master.

But don't let that stop you.

It's easy to get started. And you can get a big bang out of the basics:

- Keep a log of your problems
- Identify the A.L.E.R.T.S. associated with them
- Turn pain into power

And mentally practice with spaced repetition.

Your problem log increases awareness, helping you identify triggers. The triggers help you spot the problem before it happens. Turning pain into power gives you better options.

Mental practice, with spaced repetition, makes choosing better second nature.

With a solid plan, and the basics of priming, you now:

- Understand how weight loss works (EO < EI)
- Have a blueprint for improving your S.T.A.N.D.ing
- Make it easy to succeed & hard to fail
- With flow, engineering & mindware

Which brings us to the final leg of the bridge...

Putting it all into PRACTICE!

30

The 3rd Pillar: Practice

"The world can doubtless never be well known by theory;
practice is absolutely necessary."
–Philip Dormer Stanhope

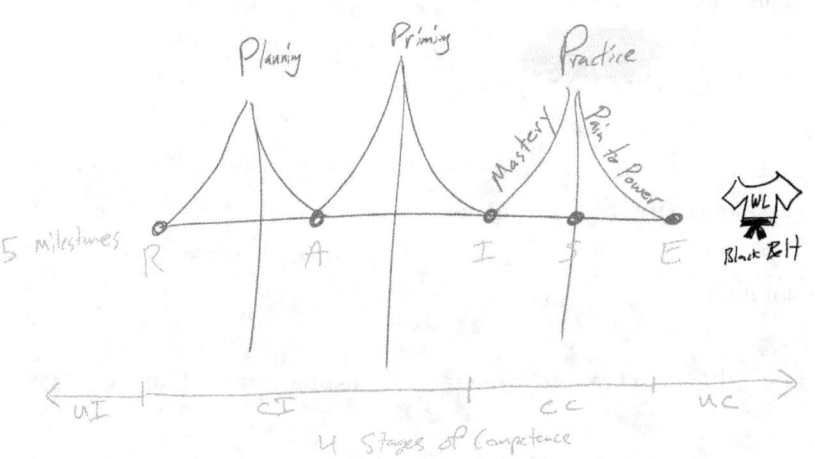

You have a plan.

You've engineered your mind & environments for success. You've optimized for flow.

Now it's time to show up and do the work.

If you're consistent, your body will improve. If you're not, it won't.

Inconsistent actions yield inconsistent results.

- You don't eat once, and become full for life...
- You don't sleep once, and become rested for life...
- You don't train once, and become strong for life..

No, you eat many times...

Sleep many times...

Train many times...

And things ONLY improve when YOU do.

Your diet improves, and you lose some weight. But to lose some more, you need to improve some more.

Not once.

Many times. Overall. It's the trend of the line, not the blip on the radar.

In other words...

CONSISTENCY MATTERS.

And yet, people say things like,

"I'm doing XYZ MOST of the time, but I'm not making any progress..."

RED ALERT!

Sound the alarms!

Whatever "MOST" means, it's not CONSISTENT enough.

Here's why...

31

Mastery: AutoMaT.I.C. Weight Loss

"The great thing in all education is to make our nervous system our ally instead of our enemy. It is to fund and capitalize our acquisitions, and live at ease upon the interest of the fund. For this we must make automatic and habitual, as early as possible, as many useful actions as we can, and as carefully guard against the growing into ways that are likely to be disadvantageous."

–William James

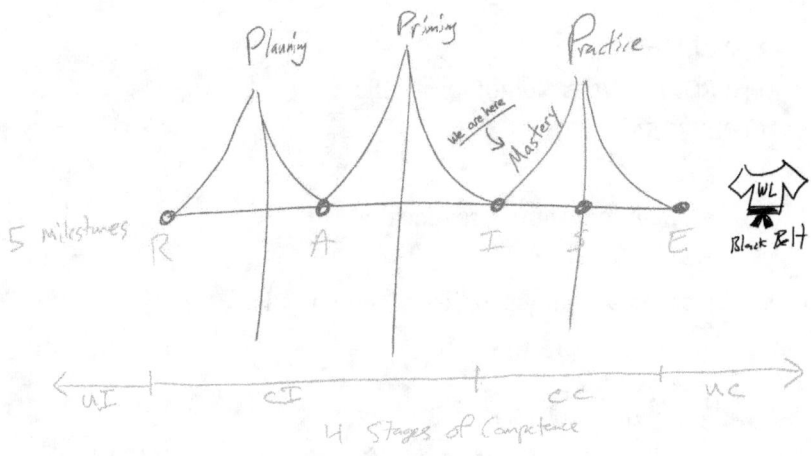

Our goal is weight loss MASTERY.

Because mastery is the stage where everything becomes easy & Auto-MaTIC.

· (Ma)stery is an
· (Auto)matic function of
· (C)onsistent
· (I)mprovements over
· (T)ime.

Or simply: **M = TIC**

This means the slower you improve, and the less consistent you are, the longer it will take to get to mastery. If time, improvement or consistency = 0, you'll NEVER become a master.

The equation for weight loss mastery is simple:

- Spend TIME
- IMPROVING your weight loss skills
- CONSISTENTLY

And you will get to weight loss BlackBelt.

This shows why so many people never get to BlackBelt.

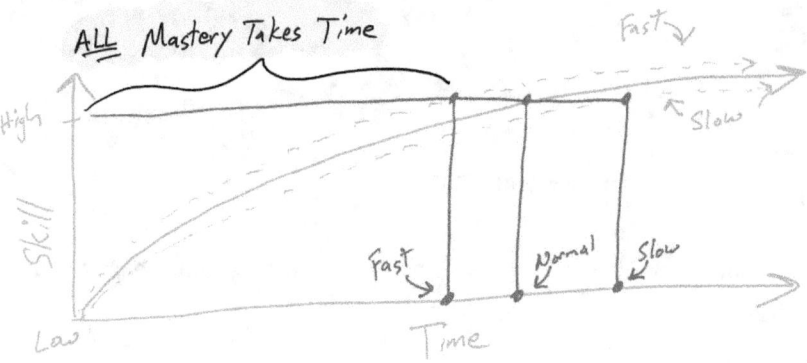

Lacking TIME

No matter how fast you lose weight, it's NEVER fast enough. But not liking the laws of physics doesn't change them. "Get the body of your dreams in 2 weeks with the diet used by [famous celebrity]" sells magazines.

But not a single one of them will deliver on the promise...

Because there isn't enough TIME.

Lacking IMPROVEMENT

You buy into the latest *"primal-paleo-ultra-low-carb-ketogenic diet..."*

And follow it to the letter.

You master it and lose weight...

Now what?

There aren't anymore carbs to cut. It didn't mention anything about sleep, training, awareness or NEPA...

Is skinny-fat without a clue as good as it gets?

Not if you keep improving...

Lacking CONSISTENCY

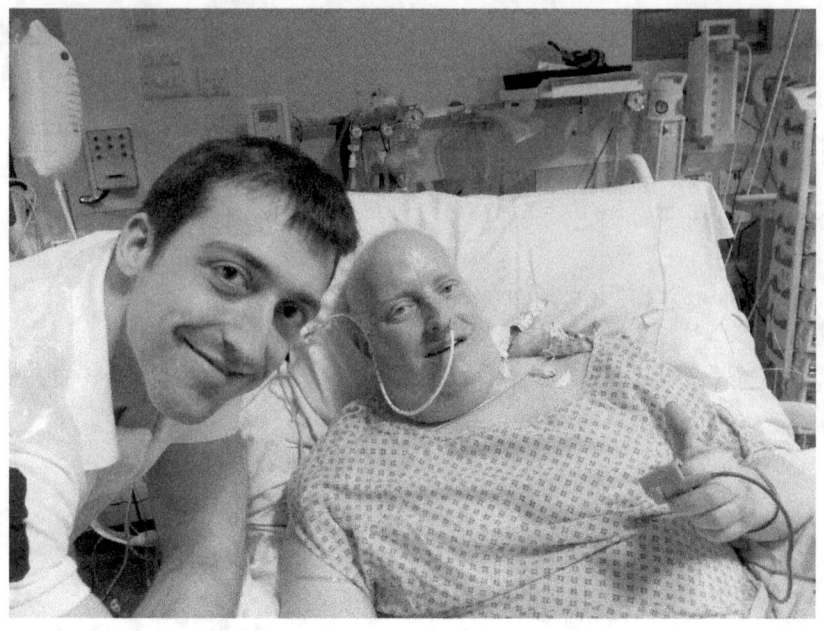

This is my friend Chris Young.

During his battle with leukemia, flesh eating bacteria devoured a quarter of his quad. He was in the ICU for MONTHS.

But even in the ICU, with tubes everywhere, a big chunk of his leg gone, bed sores & unable to wiggle his toes...

He trained.

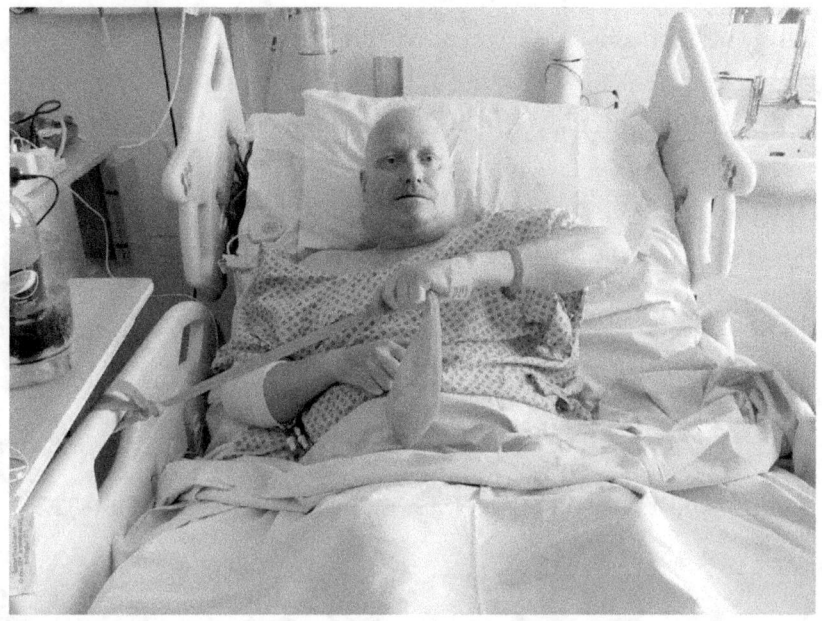

His motto was, "if you have the mind to train, you'll find a way."

And so he did.

You wouldn't know it from the photo, but he was one of the strongest men on the planet...

A world record holder in powerlifting.

He was a champion because he had the mind, and consistency, of a champion. Whether you're a complete beginner, or the strongest in the world...

<u>You can always show up</u>, and put in a good effort.

But if you're inconsistent, you have a problem.

William James tells us,

"Each lapse is like the letting fall of a ball of string which one is carefully winding up: a single slip undoes more than a great many turns will wind again."

When this happens, it doesn't matter what plan you're following. You're not going to look or feel any better long-term...

Because you're not being CONSISTENT enough to get PERSISTENT results.

So if you want to get to weight loss BlackBelt:

· Start SMALL
· Improve your skills
· Be consistent

And let time take care of itself.

Do this, and you'll be lean for life before you know it.

Question: What about flexibility?

How can you be 100% consistent & flexible at the same time?

Answer: Make demands so small, 100% consistency isn't "inflexible."

Think of it like this...

Pretend you're an author. If you ALWAYS write at least 1 sentence a day, you'll complete a novel every 8 years on average.

That's the WORST case.

But when one sentence turns into 2, 10, or 100... you complete your novel in 2 years instead of 8. Or a weekend instead of a lifetime, like my last book.

When I say flexible, I mean "flexible within reason."

One sentence a day shouldn't lower your quality of life. And if it does, you shouldn't be an author.

100% consistency deals with minimums (for healthy behaviors) and maximums (for harmful behaviors).

Here are some S.T.A.N.D.-Up examples:

- SLEEP: I _always_ stop watching TV after midnight
- TRAINING: I _always_ train at least twice a week
- AWARENESS: I _never_ avoid logging my food or problems
- NEPA: I _always_ do 5 minutes of NEPA in the morning
- DIET: I _never_ have more than 10 alcoholic drinks in a day

These aren't GREEN behaviors, but the 100% consistency moves you in the right direction.

Inconsistency doesn't.

M = TIC

Improve consistently, and results will follow.

From the spring in your step, to the weight on the scale... and the smile looking back at you in the mirror.

- Engineer for consistency.
- Log your problems as they come.

And turn pain, into power...

32

Pain to Power

"Problems worthy of attack prove their worth by hitting back."
–Piet Hein

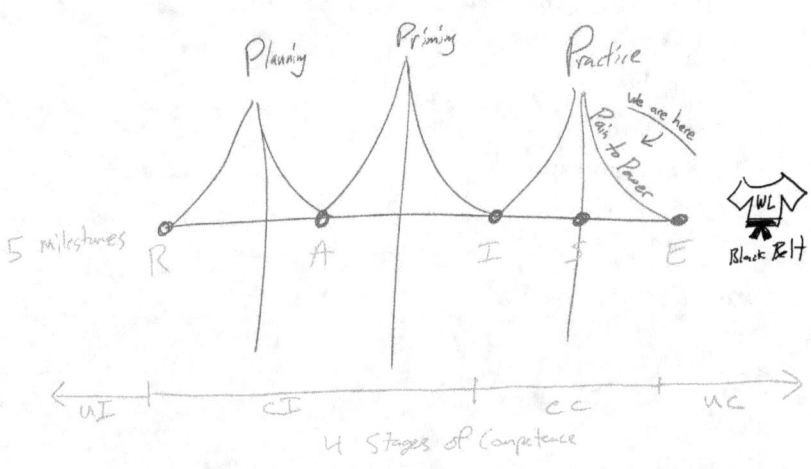

Things were going so well...

- You discovered you knowledge gaps
- Got your head wrapped around energy balance
- Found a proven blueprint for success
- Stopped focusing on the scale
- Started focusing on body composition
- Optimized for flow

And started engineering your mind and environments for success.

It became easier and easier to succeed.

Harder and harder to fail...

But not impossible.

One day, you experience dietary Chernobyl... a chain of events which leads to you caving in and eating:

- An entire bucket of ice cream
- A bag of Doritos
- A bowl of spicy ramen
- A box of Oreos

And washing them down with:

- Milk
- Beer
- Coca-Cola

Then you head to bed...

A few minutes pass. And you start seeing yourself from a 3rd person perspective. You think to yourself, "Aren't I a clumsy bastard?" As you watch yourself get out of bed...

Stumble to the bathroom...

And spend the rest of the night on the floor. Hugging and singing sweet serenades to your porceline God.

Death stops by to say, "Hi!"

But your state is so pitiful, he decides to leave you alone.

And let you live a little longer...

Hoping you'll learn from your mistakes...

And DO better.

Oh, wait... **that was ME.**

Not you.

But maybe you've done something similarly stupid.

And if you have...

No big deal.

That's right, **"NO BIG DEAL!"**

As terrible as your mistakes may be, the real tragedy isn't screwing up...

It's FAILING to LEARN.

Problems are nothing more than opportunities in disguise. And when you learn from them, they make you better. Ray Dalio says, "View painful problems as potential improvements that are SCREAMING at you."

When something is screaming at you, what do you do?

- Run TOWARDS it? (fight)
- Run AWAY from it? (flight)

If they're YOUR problems...

You CAN'T run away from them.

There's only one option.

FIGHT!

Federich Chopin says,

"Every difficulty slurred over will be a ghost to disturb your repose later on."

You don't want the same ghosts (pains & problems) haunting you, over and over, until the day you die. So instead of avoiding reality, you're going to confront it.

Turn your PAIN into POWER.

It starts by keeping a problem log:

- Keep a log of your problems
- Especially the most painful ones

Whenever you're in pain (physically or emotionally), take notes.

- How are you feeling?
- What triggered the pain? (A.L.E.R.T.S. - coming soon)
- Why you don't want to feel this way again in the future?

For some people, this will take tremendous courage.

If you're not there yet, consider getting help from a clinical psychologist. A good one will be able to help you more than any book.

Otherwise, start logging.

Most of the time, the fight isn't as hard as you think.

Seneca observes,

"We are more often frightened than hurt; and we suffer more from imagination than from reality."

This happens because your brain, among other things, is a simulation machine.

And those who struggle with weight loss often forecast inaccurate simulations.

For example...

Simulation #1: Visualizing Failure → Inaction

- Person simulates weight loss
- They see themselves fail
- So they never try
- Chance of success = 0%

Simulation #2: Visualizing Success → Action

- Person simulates weight loss
- They see themselves succeed
- So they get started
- Chance of success > 0%

Simulation #3: Visualizing Failure → Acting Anyway

- Person simulates weight loss
- They see themselves fail
- But they don't confuse simulations with reality
- So they try anyway
- Chance of success > 0%

Our brains are powerful tools, but they don't come with manuals. The natural thing to do is trust the little voice in your head. And the simulations your brain produces.

But the voice in your head, and your mental simulations can be misleading. They're part of your thinking process...

But they're not "YOU."

You have the power to override them.

And it starts by seeing them for what they are...

Simulations.

NOT reality.

My friend Becky couldn't visualize success when she was first starting out...

But now she's lost over 150 lbs...

More important than visualizing success, is getting started.

Because the only way you're guaranteed to fail, is if you never try.

You can start by logging your "problems."

They're your biggest opportunities moving forward.

And once you know what they are, you can fix them.

III

The "How" of Weight Loss

33

Milestone 4: Stagnation

"Everyone has a plan till they get punched in the mouth."
–Mike Tyson

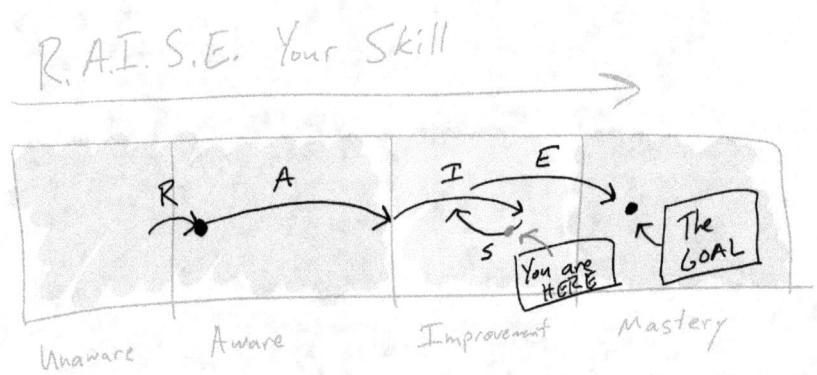

The needle on the scale is going down, down, down...

Then one day, it stops.

Reverses.

And starts moving in the wrong direction!

You've reached the 4th milestone...

STAGNATION.

This point is critical.

It will determine whether all your work up to this point was all in vain, or the best investment of your life...

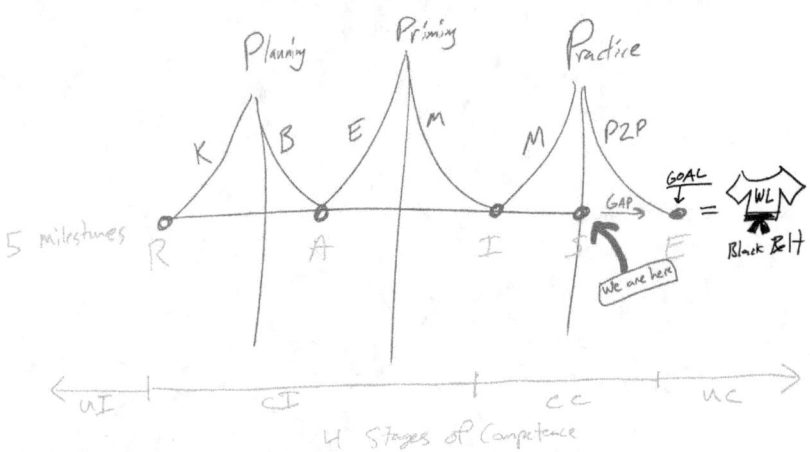

You're on the final leg of the bridge.

And just need to turn this pain (plateau) into power.

Here's why you're stuck, and what to do about it...

34

Expectations vs. Reality

"If you tell me that you desire a fig, I answer you that there must be time.
Let it first blossom, then bear fruit, then ripen."
–Epictetus

Stagnation is normal.

But it catches many people by surprise.

Many people think weight loss looks like this:

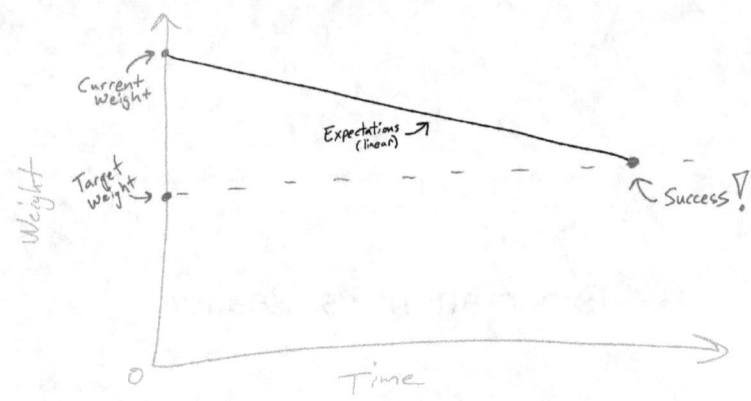

But in reality, it's full of ups & downs:

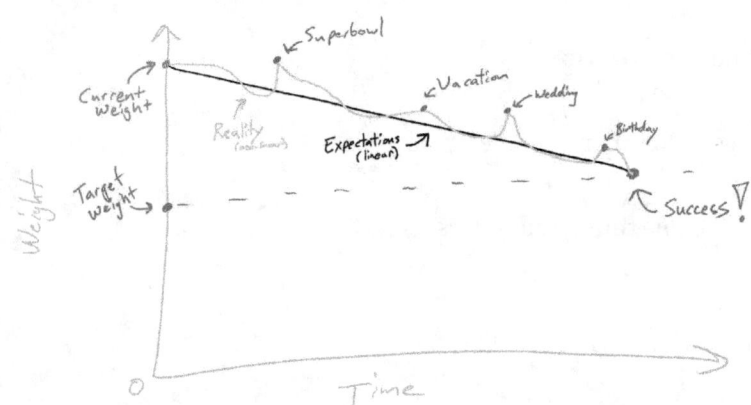

It's a roller coaster!

As you can see, your weight WILL fluctuate.

But as long as you keep improving your skills...

Don't worry.

You'll get to your goal.

Whenever your weight:

- Goes up 10 lbs in one night
- Goes down 10 lbs in one week

It's not fat.

This will feel like good news if your weight goes up. And bad news if your weight goes down. These are fluctuations in <u>WATER weight</u>.

It's frustrating, but normal.

The simple fact is... you body doesn't change that fast.

But over time, it WILL change.

Your new skills overpower your old habits.

And the fat comes off.

I don't expect you to weigh yourself daily. If you do, great. But it's more important to weigh yourself every 2-3 weeks, under the same conditions.

If the longer trend line isn't going down, then you have a problem.

When this happens, you want to either:

1. Take your current skills up a notch
2. Or start developing a new skill

A big reason many people get stuck is because they don't develop new skills.

Instead of seeking more quick-wins, they chase ever diminishing returns...

Not smart.

For example, pretend you're spending 3 hours weight training each week. Doubling your training to 6 hours won't do much. But starting a food log, if you don't keep one, will take MINUTES a day.

AND give you better results, faster.

Don't major in the minors.

Get to baseline in all 5 skills (S.T.A.N.D.) before chasing diminishing returns.

We've covered the skills specific to weight loss.

Now we'll look at the skills specific to the 7 plateaus.

And how to break through them...

35

The 7 Plateaus

"The block of granite which was an obstacle on the pathway of the weak, becomes a stepping stone on the pathway of the strong."
–Thomas Carlyle

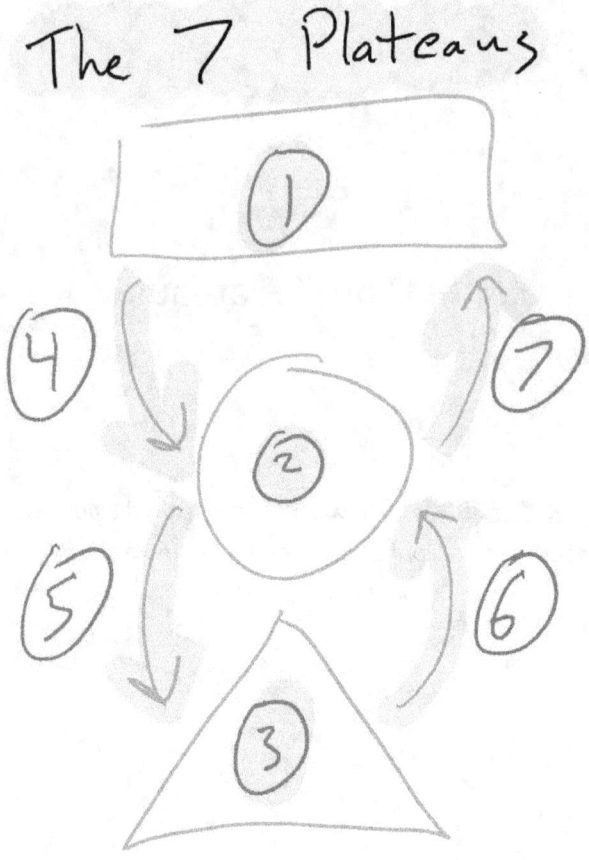

PLATEAU #1: Concept

You've read the headlines. One week, eggs are going to kill you. The next week, they're heart healthy...

What gives?!

PLATEAU #2: Mindset

You go to the gym 4 times a week, train your ass off, and don't lose a single pound...

Why bother working out if nothing you do makes a dent?

PLATEAU #3: Action

You count every calorie.

You weigh every gram of food, and measure every ounce of liquid. You ensure you have a 500kcal/day deficit. You SHOULD be losing at least 1lb/week...

But the scale doesn't budge.

What's going on?!

Thanks to the work of Karl Popper, there's an easy way to understand and solve these problems.

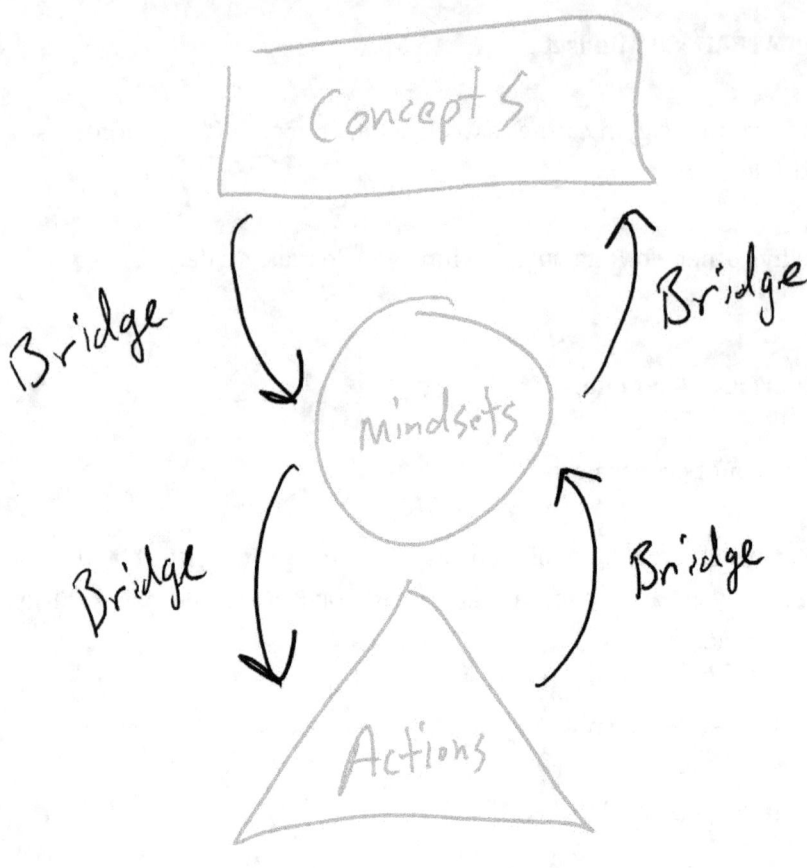

Your problems fit into 1 of 3 "worlds."

- Concepts – how you abstract, associate & store information
- Mindsets – how you frame, focus & interpret information
- Actions – what your physical body does in the world

If you're familiar with Descarte's mind–body dualism, you can think of it as:

- Inner World: Concepts & Mindsets

- Outer World: Actions

Popper looked at the mind as a bridge between the reality (actions) and the abstract (concepts). When you suffer, it's because of harmful concepts, mindsets and actions...

OR because one or more of your bridges are broken.

In the calorie counting example earlier... you may THINK you're getting a 500 kcal/day deficit. But in reality, you're not.

You may have adopted a false concept. For example, you memorized the wrong nutrition info for a common food. If you're eating TWICE the calories you think, you can easily offset your daily deficit.

Maybe it's a mindset issue and you're not counting some calories. This could be intentionally for "reasons" or unintentionally because you simply forget. Either way, a harmful mindset is interfering with your weight loss.

Or it could be your actions.

Maybe your scale isn't calibrated well, so you under-weigh all your food.

These are 3 of the 7 ways to go wrong.

And any one of them can stop your progress dead in its tracks...

DESPITE your best efforts.

Because of this, research shows people regularly underestimate what they eat by as much as 40%. This EASILY offsets a 500 kcal deficit...

If you're near the 40% range, you may GAIN weight instead of losing it.

Despite THINKING you should be getting leaner...

See how this could be a problem?

Your concepts, mindsets & actions range from plagued to powerful. And the states of the 4 bridges connecting them either amplify or diminish their power.

When you hit a weight loss plateau, it's because there's a problem in one or more of these 7 places. Broken bridges and plagued worlds make it impossible to get lean.

To get the scale moving again, you need to:

- Cure the plagues
- And fix the bridges

Once you do, the problems (and your extra fat) fade away...

36

3 Worlds, 3 Plagues

"The hell to be endured hereafter, of which theology tells, is no worse than the hell we make for ourselves in this world by habitually fashioning our characters in the wrong way. "
-William James

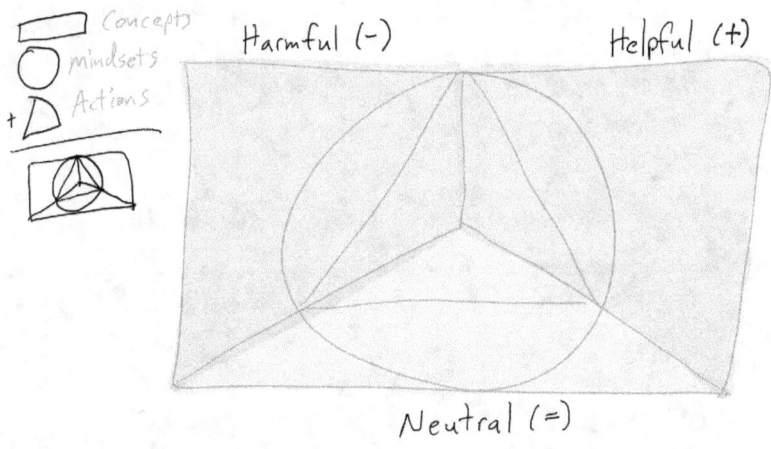

There are 3 plagues stopping your weight loss dead in its tracks:

1. FALSE Concepts
2. FIXED Mindsets
3. FLAWED Actions

FALSE CONCEPTS have you expecting one thing, and getting another.

FIXED MINDSETS stop you from tapping into your full potential.

FLAWED ACTIONS give you meager, or even negative results.

To get & stay lean for life, you need to make all 3 worlds healthy.

And it starts with the right MINDSETS...

37

The 1st Plague

"Since we cannot change reality,
let us change the eyes which see reality."
-Nikos Kazantzakis

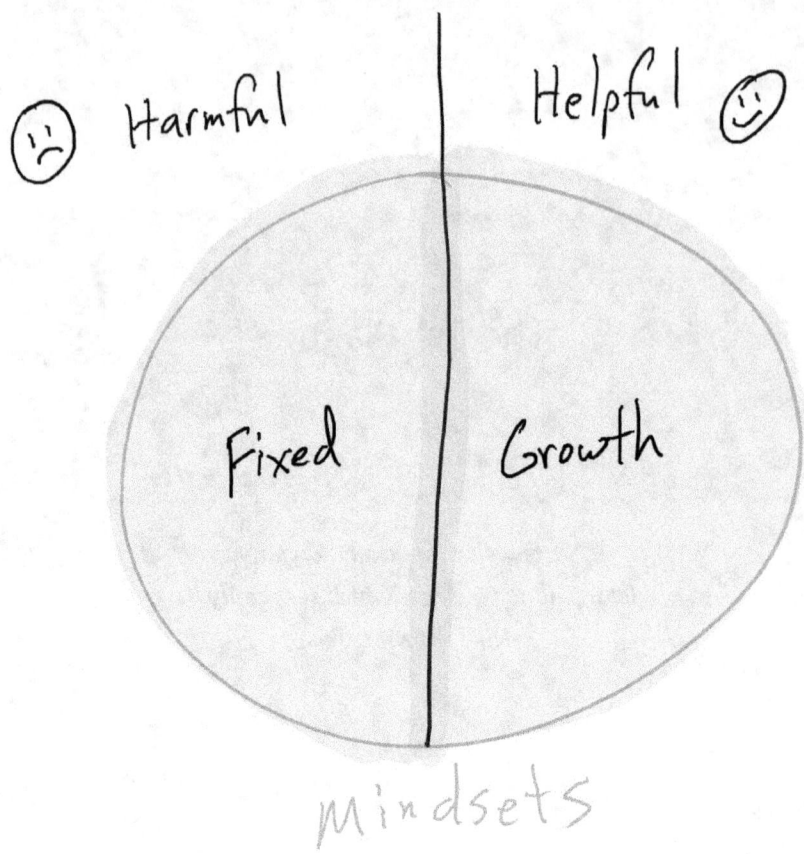

Harmful   Helpful

Fixed   Growth

Mindsets

MINDSETS are:

- HELPFUL when they promote GROWTH
- HARMFUL when they lead to STAGNATION

Carol Dweck refers to these as FIXED and GROWTH mindsets in her excellent book, "Mindset." Mindsets are simply beliefs.

And your beliefs matter!

To see why, let's compare "Fixed (mindset) Freddy" (FF) to people with growth mindsets.

Who do you think performs better in the face of...?

SETBACKS

FF: "I gave it a shot..." (and didn't do well, so I gave up)

vs. *"Winners never quit, and quitters never win."* –Jim Rohn

I thought I'd write this book in a week. But due to setbacks, it's approaching 2 months. The only reason you're able to read this page is because I persisted.

CHALLENGES

FF: "It looks pretty hard..." (so I won't try)

vs. *"Little by little, a little becomes a lot."* –Tanzanian Proverb

The easiest way to lose 80 lbs is to lose one pound, eighty times.

80lbs is a big scary challenge. 1lb isn't.

SOCIAL COMPARISON

FF: "I'm not a natural..." (so no point in trying)

vs. *"You have complete control of your life. F*ck the genetics." -Neil deGrasse Tyson*

I wasn't a jock in school.

I was a weak, fat nerd who played video games. And went to the bowling alley instead of prom. I used to think, "I'll never be strong like those guys."

And didn't touch a weight until I was 22.

But by the time I was 25, people started calling me a "jock."

Wha… who… me?!

With a few years of weight training, my strength soared. My deadlift went from non-existent to nearly 600lbs. Not what you'd expect from a weak video game nerd who, "will never be strong."

F*ck the genetics.

EFFORT

FF: "It's not worth my time…" (so I won't bother)

vs. *"Genius is an infinite capacity for taking pains." -Thomas Carlyle*

At one point in my life, I was:

- Weighing & counting all my calories

- Packing ALL my food so I could hit specific macros
- Taking about $200 worth of supplements/month
- Waking up at 2 AM to drink a protein shake
- Running intervals for an hour every morning

And training 8x a week...

DESPITE coughing up blood every morning after my run due to air pollution (about which I was CLUELESS at the time — a Minnesota boy who'd taken clean air for granted).

I did far too much, for much too little.

My actions were wrong, but my mindset was right...

I was willing to put in the effort.

FEEDBACK

FF: "He's an idiot..." (so I won't learn from him)

vs. *"Take what is useful. Discard what is not. Add what is uniquely your own."* *-Bruce Lee*

People think they're natural-born experts on 3 things:

1. Politics
2. Religion
3. Weight Loss

Whether you want others opinions or not, you're going to get them. So you might as well be graceful, and hear them out. And use their words to:

- Remind you of what you know to be true
- Remind you of what you know to be false
- Identify knowledge gaps you need to fill
- Identify updates for your mental models

Here's a quick summary:

	Fixed	Growth
Setbacks	"I gave it a shot..." (but gave up easily)	"Winners never quit, and quitters never win." -Jim Rohn
Challenges	"It's looks pretty hard..." (so I won't try)	"Little by little, a little becomes a lot." -Tanzanian Proverb
Comparison to others	"I'm not a natural..." (so no point in trying)	"You have complete control of your life. F*ck the genetics." -Neil deGrasse Tyson
Effort	"It's not worth my time..." (so I won't bother)	"Genius is an infinite capacity for taking pains." -Thomas Carlyle
Feedback	"He's an idiot..." (so I won't learn from him)	"Take what is useful. Discard what is not. Add what is uniquely your own." -Bruce Lee

Growth mindsets lead to greatness. And fixed mindsets lead to failure.

Fixed Freddy won't get lean with his current mindsets.

But luckily, he can change them.

Because mindsets are just beliefs. Fixed mindsets are known as "limiting beliefs" because they hold you back from better outcomes.

So if you find yourself plagued by any of the fixed mindsets above...

Change them.

It'll take time. Your mental simulations of the future may be fuzzy or negative. When they are, ignore them.

Try anyway.

As Henry Ford said, *"Whether you think you can, or can't... you're right."*

38

The 2nd Plague

"The truth will set you free, but first it will make you miserable."
−James A. Garfield

CONCEPTS are:

- HELPFUL when ACCURATE
- HARMFUL when INACCURATE

Consider "calories don't count."

If you understood the fundamental concept of weight loss (EI < EO), you know calories DO count. So "calories don't count" is inaccurate. And if believed, leads dieters to other INACCURATE conclusions, such as...

"healthy" = "good for weight loss"

Chains of causal logic based on false premises lead to problems in making sense of reality.

For example, let's pretend you snack on nuts all day ad libitum (as much as you want).

You do this because you think:

- Nuts are a great healthy snack
- Calories don't count

After months of this "healthy" snacking, you gain 10lbs.

You wonder:

- Am I genetically broken?
- Am I doing something wrong?

No and no.

You're doing everything right, based on your concept. And you would be WILDLY successful IF your concept were right...

But it isn't.

You're acting on a FALSE concept. So you don't get the results you expect.

The problem is:

- **Calories DO count**
- And nuts have LOADS of them!

You're eating too many damn nuts to create the energy deficit you need to lose weight.

Once you realize this, the fix is simple:

- Stop eating so many nuts
- Start losing weight

When a statement isn't 100% accurate, you want to:

- Find a simpler concept which is more accurate (think Occam's razor)
- Learn the concept inside-out (common nuances & exceptions)

Luckily, a simple & accurate concept DOES exist for weight loss.

It's called energy balance.

This will help jog your memory:

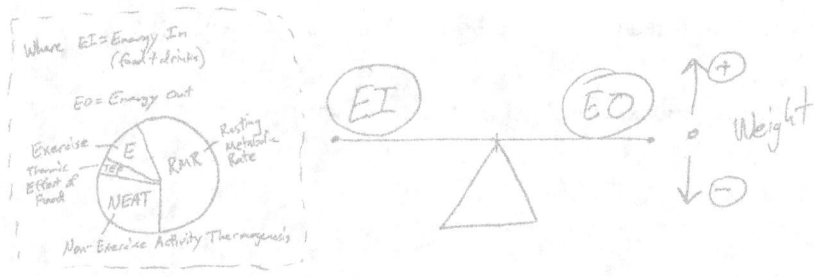

As long as you create a net energy deficit over time (regardless of what you eat), you WILL lose weight.

"The Twinkie Diet" is an excellent example (search Google).

You might FEEL better if you eat healthier foods. You may be more satiated.

But if you're overweight and not getting leaner...

You can't claim to be eating "healthy."

Most people say "healthy" meaning "good for health." But being overweight is "bad for health." So if your diet is causing you to keep/gain weight, it's NOT healthy.

"Healthy eating" doesn't cause weight loss...

But energy deficits DO.

Concepts which are 100% accurate are hard to find.

They exist on a spectrum, from 0 - 100%. Most of the time you'll encounter low accuracy concepts in popular diet books. These are over-simplified (Occam's lobotomy), and not very helpful.

In quality books, you'll get higher accuracy.

But this comes at a cost.

To be accurate, there are more nuances. And because of this, they're less likely to gain popularity.

This is why the celebrity diet spreads...

And the hidden gem stays hidden.

Like this book. I don't expect it will become popular. If it does, it'll be one of those popular books everyone loves, but few people read.

I've written as simply and accurately as I'm able... but this is NOT easy reading. The only reason you're still here is because you don't give up when the going gets tough.

And that's a great mindset to have!

Keep going.

Because if you want success in weight loss (or any other area of life)...

You want ACCURACY.

With the right concepts and mindsets, the last place for screw-ups is at the point of execution...

39

The 3rd Plague

"Success is simple. Do what's right, the right way, at the right time."
–Arnold H. Glasow

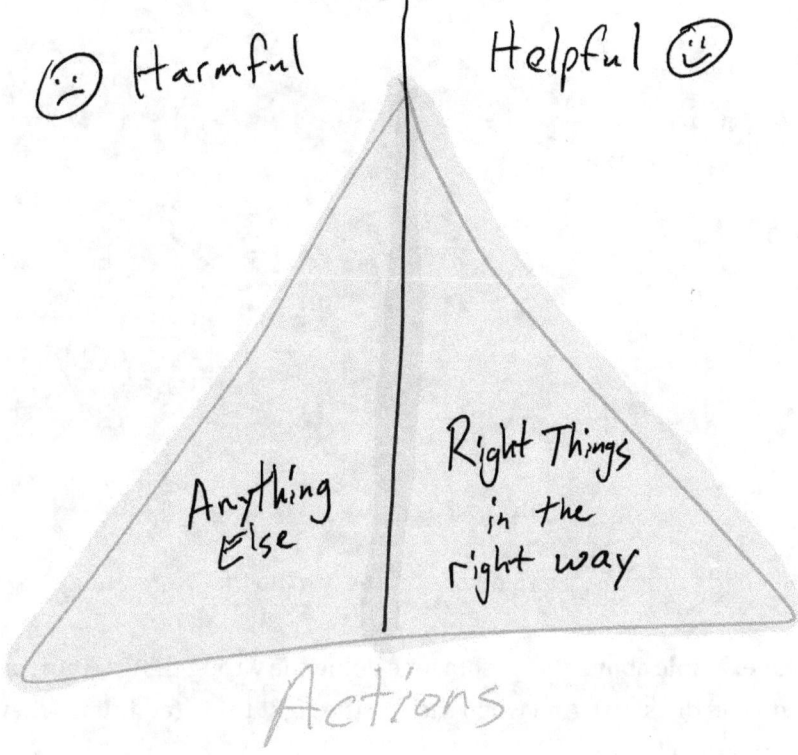

ACTIONS are:

- HELPFUL when you're doing the RIGHT things in the RIGHT way (at the right time)
- HARMFUL when doing anything else

Here's why it's so easy to screw-up:

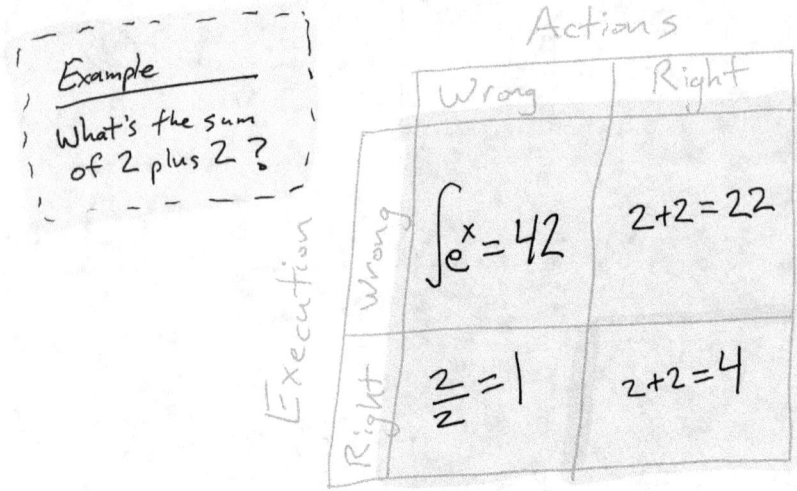

When it's time to act as a novice, it's easy to do the wrong things.

Our example above shows someone doing the wrong things (integration and division). And when they do the right thing (addition), they do it wrong (2+2=22).

There are infinite ways to go wrong, and few ways to go right.

I'm sure you've seen this before in weight loss:

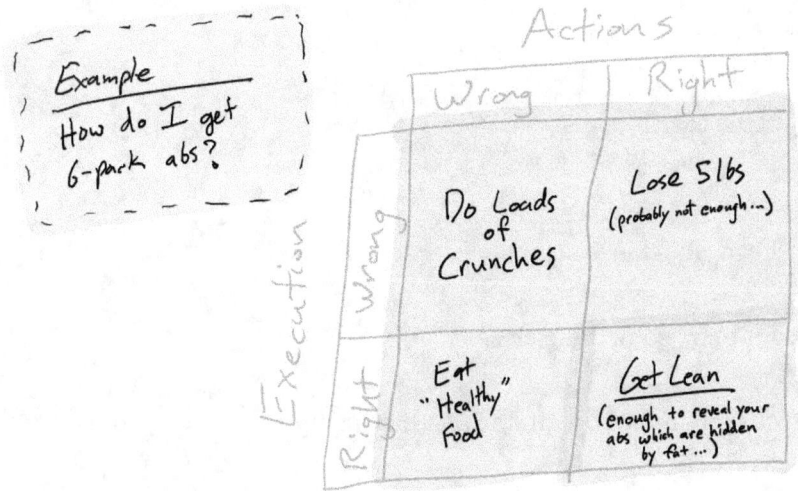

When you spend 20 years teaching math, you learn a few things:

- Those who master the fundamentals progress easily
- Those who don't, struggle
- There are infinite ways to get the WRONG answer
- Before students know the answer, some problems seem "impossible"
- Once students know the answer, "impossible" becomes "obvious"

And the same is true in weight loss.

"Those who master the fundamentals progress easily."

Get to weight loss baseline.

It's only 5 skills.

The better your S.T.A.N.D.ing, the better you look...

And the easier it gets.

"Those who don't, struggle"

Want to try something else?

Focus on things other than S.T.A.N.D.ing up?

It may take months, years or decades to discover...

But I can virtually guarantee you'll be wasting time & effort.

EVERYTHING else you do will take longer and be less effective.

"There are infinite ways to get the WRONG answer"

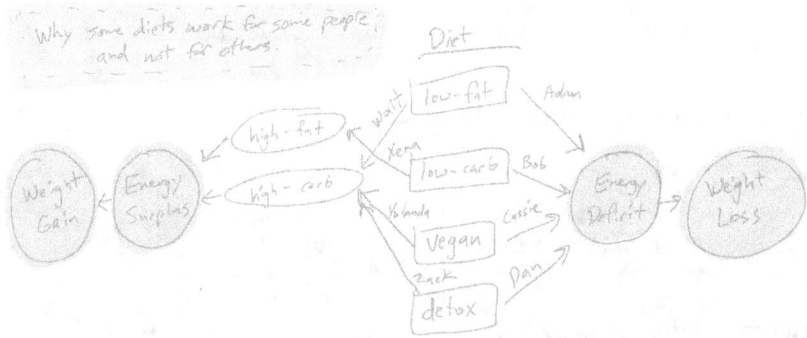

Adam tries a low-fat diet and loses weight.

- He concludes fat makes you fat.
- And recommends low-fat diets for weight loss.

Bob tries a low-carb diet and loses weight.

- He concludes carbs make you fat.
- And recommends low-carb diets for weight loss.

Cassie tries a vegan diet and loses weight.

- She concludes animal products make you fat.
- And recommends vegan diets for weight loss.

Dan tries a detox diet and loses weight.

- He concludes "toxins" make you fat.
- And recommends detoxing for weight loss.

(person) tries (fad diet) and loses weight.

- (person) concludes (inaccuracy)
- And recommends (suboptimal actions) for weight loss

Sometimes, people do the right things for the wrong reasons.

A common example is your friend losing weight on the Paleo diet.

You ask what they do. And they tell you, "paleo."

So you "go paleo."

But you don't lose weight.

Your friend says,

- "You must be doing something wrong."
- "It works. Don't be stupid."
- "No seriously, WTF is wrong with you?"

But the truth is, THEY have it wrong.

Not you.

Energy deficits cause weight loss.

NOT paleo, keto, low-fat, low-carb, elimination, cyclic, detox or any other nonsense.

If the author pretends "calories don't count," it's bunkum.

Any of these diets CAN cause weight loss INDIRECTLY. But to be efficient & effective, our goal is ACCURACY.

For this, energy deficits fit the bill, while paleo myths don't.

"Before students know the answer, some problems seem 'impossible'"

Some problems may still feel impossible, but...

"Once students know the answer, 'impossible' problems become 'easy'"

Adam says, "How did this ever used to be hard?"

If you've plateaued, one or more of your worlds is likely plagued by:

· FIXED mindsets
· INACCURATE concepts

- FLAWED actions

To cure the plague(s), you need to:

- Embrace GROWTH mindsets
- Increase the ACCURACY of your knowledge
- Do the RIGHT things in the RIGHT way (at the right time)

Most dieters have no idea how much of the big picture they're missing. The problems we've discussed seem random. They don't see the pattern, so they don't address the root cause.

And they keep repeating the same mistakes:

- They diet hop (low carb/fat/meat)
- They do the wrong things for abs (crunches, belts, pills)
- They develop fixed mindsets (not worth it, too hard, I'm broken)

Because of this, they never see the light at the end of the tunnel...

And give up.

But not you. You have a blueprint for the right concepts, mindsets & actions.

We just need to get rid of the R.A.T.S...

40

4 Dirty R.A.T.S.

"In theory there is nothing to hinder our following what we are taught; but in life there are many things to draw us aside."
−Epictetus

Your 3 worlds are healthy.

You've cured the plagues.

Armed with:

- Accurate concepts
- Growth mindsets
- Right actions

You'd EXPECT to be losing weight, right?

I mean, what else could POSSIBLY go wrong?!

HAVING tools isn't the same as USING them.

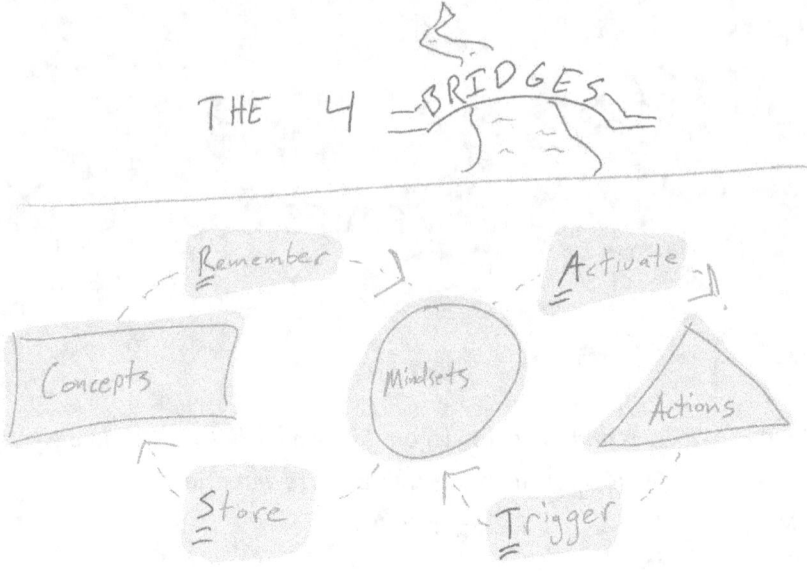

The bridges between your 3 worlds can have gaps:

- Failure to (R)emember the right things at the right times
- Failure to (A)ct on what you know you should do
- Failure to (T)rigger the right responses when cued
- Failure to (S)tore accurate knowledge in long term memory

These dirty R.A.T.S. create GAPS in your 4 bridges.

And cause the following:

- You KNOW better than you SHOW
- You SHOULD do better, but don't
- You set the alarm, but don't hear it ring

- You forget faster than you can remember

Wouldn't it be nice if you remembered the right things at the right times?

So you don't waste countless hours reinventing the wheel...

Like eating your veggies before they spoil in the fridge. Bringing your gym bag to the gym, instead of forgetting it at home. And getting to bed on time instead of groaning through life like a sleep-deprived zombie...

What if you USED all your "life-changing ideas" instead of forgetting them?

Or never "getting around" to it...

I haven't met a single dieter who doesn't "KNOW BETTER."

Not one.

But I've met many who fail to DO BETTER.

The key to DOING better is to:

- Fix your bridges
- And keep them in good repair

When you do, NOTHING can stop you.

41

The 1st Bridge

"Everyone has a photographic memory. Some just don't have film."
–Stephen Wright

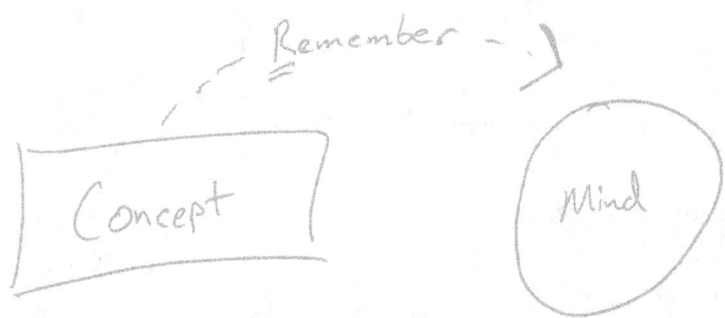

Imagine we're sitting down at the Original Pancake House (OPH) for breakfast. I order my go-to meal...

The lumberjack breakfast.

A gigantic bowl filled with eggs, bacon, sausage gravy, cheese, hash browns and biscuits.

I ask for extra:

- Gravy
- Butter
- Blueberry pancakes

Eating a day and a half's worth of food in one sitting is a problem. It doesn't matter who you are. But, as I teach my clients, there's a simple fix.

You can:

- Enjoy your meal
- Many times
- For the same cost
- With fewer calories

By putting 2/3 of it into a to-go box before you eat it.

Instead of gorging on calorie-dense food until your buttons pop, you enjoy your food now AND later...

WITHOUT having to worry about gaining weight.

Simple enough, right?

If only you could REMEMBER to get that to-go box BEFORE it's too late...

We have 3 problems with remembering:

- Failing to STORE information
- Failing to TRIGGER retrieval at the right time
- Failing to RETRIEVE stored information when you want it

Pretend you go to OPH on your own, with intent to box-up part of your gigantic breakfast in a to-go box. The information is top of mind...

Until you get a text message.

Then the waitress comes as you're responding. You put the phone down, and order your meal. While you're waiting, you think,

"What am I forgetting?"

Your meal comes.

You devour the whole thing.

Then it hits you...

"I FORGOT THE TO-GO BOX!"

You start stomping and cursing like Yosemite Sam.

This is what happens when:

- · Your STORAGE worked (the concept was there)
- · Your TRIGGERS worked (you wanted to retrieve something)

But your RETRIEVAL failed (you couldn't remember WHAT you needed).

No big deal.

Throw it in your problem log.

And create mindware to turn your PAIN into POWER.

Once you fix your memory bridge, forgetting will be a problem of the past. It's something we can fix.

But even with a perfect memory, you're not in the clear.

Let's pretend you go to OPH again.

And this time you REMEMBER to get a to-go box...

But don't ask for one.

This is a failure to ACTIVATE.

It's not enough to KNOW better...

You must DO better.

42

The 2nd Bridge

"Stop shoulding all over yourself."
–Tony Robbins

Have you ever experienced the following?

- Your bedtime alarm goes off. You *should* go to bed, but don't.
- You *should* eat veggies with your meal, but don't.
- You *should* ask for a to-go box, but don't.
- You *should* go to the gym, but don't...

BJ Fogg's behavior model does an excellent job of explaining WHY we fail to do what we "should."

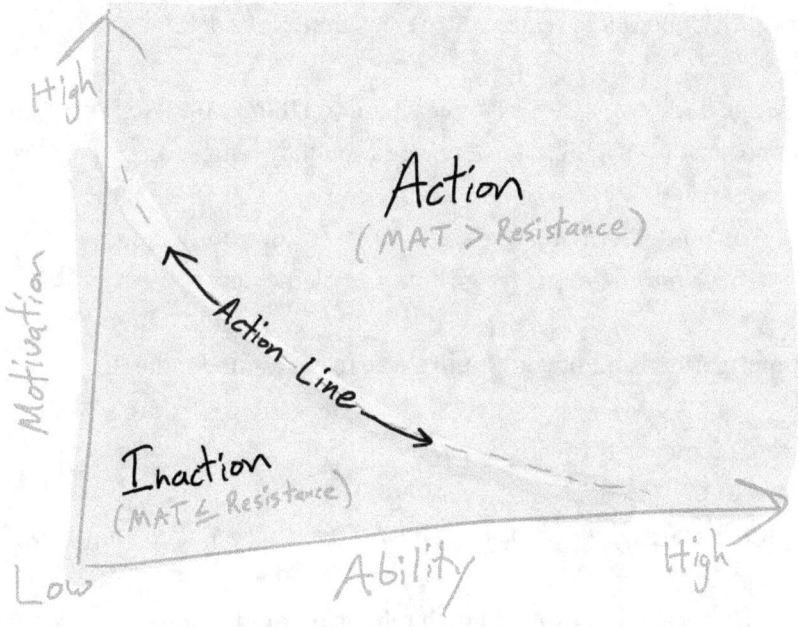

The formula for ACTIVATING (taking action) is:

B=MAT

Where:

- B = behavior

- M = motivation
- A = ability
- T = trigger

You take action (B) when MAT > resistance (action line).

- When motivation is high, you can do almost anything
- When ability is high, motivation doesn't matter as much
- When you fail to trigger (T=0), you don't take action

If we go back to our OPH example where you REMEMBER to ask for the to-go box (T > 0), there are 2 reasons you may not get one:

- You don't WANT to save some for later (low motivation)
- They don't have any to-go boxes available (low ability)

If motivation is high, you'll find a way to eat a smaller meal.

Even if it means throwing 2/3 away.

As Nietzsche says, *"He who has a WHY to live can bear almost any HOW."*

But there's a major problem with relying on motivation...

It WANES over time.

To combat this, most coaches I know try to boost motivation by encouraging you to:

- Remember your "WHY"
- Watch inspirational videos

- Put inspirational posters on your wall
- Join a group with the same goals as you
- Plan for setbacks & how you will get past them

And these work... for a while.

But not forever.

Like the opening song in "Friends," you have a bad day, week, month or year...

Except unlike the song, nobody's there for you.

You doubt your WHY.

The videos don't inspire you. The posters depress you. Your training group disbands. Or kicks you out. You go to a deep, dark place.

Your setbacks seem insurmountable.

Because motivation wanes, like willpower, it's a TERRIBLE long-term strategy.

Short-term, it moves mountains.

And in the beginning, it's all you have...

Or is it?

43

When Motivation Wanes...

"First say to yourself what you would be;
and then do what you have to do."
–Epictetus

At LimitSlayer.com we distinguish between limit SLAYERS and limit SLAVES.

Most dieters are SLAVES to motivation. They do everything they can in their power to "get pumped up." It feels good when it's there.

And in the beginning, it's all they have.

But in the long run, tying your success to motivation is a recipe for disaster.

What if, instead of relying on motivation forever, you:

- Harness it in the beginning, when it's strongest
- And use it to build the SKILLS you'll need later when it wanes...

Look at the graph again:

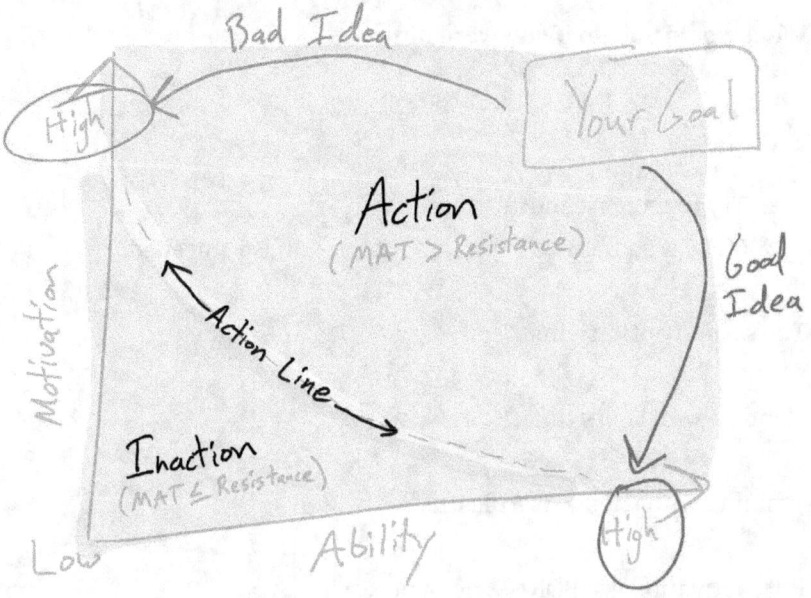

How can you take action when motivation is low?

By increasing your ABILITY to activate.

My friend lost 80 pounds recently.

He also got a new job. And when he did, he lost the ability to train with his group. He LOVED his training partners.

But he lost them due to his new hours.

His motivation plummeted. He's in a slump, and doesn't want to train alone. He's not going to the gym as regularly anymore.

And the weight is creeping back.

What would you do if you were him?

Would you:

1. Try to increase motivation?
2. Make it so EASY to train that motivation isn't needed?

The second option wins.

Hands down. Every time.

Training with friends is a blast.

But motivation is a BONUS, not a necessity.

Most of my training years, I trained alone. Nobody to motivate me when I didn't feel like it. Nobody to look forward to seeing.

Just me and the iron.

Rain or shine.

For 13 years and counting...

By increasing your ABILITY, you get to the point where it doesn't matter if you FEEL like going to the gym or not.

You go anyway.

You MAKE it fun.

It's good for you.

And that's "reason enough."

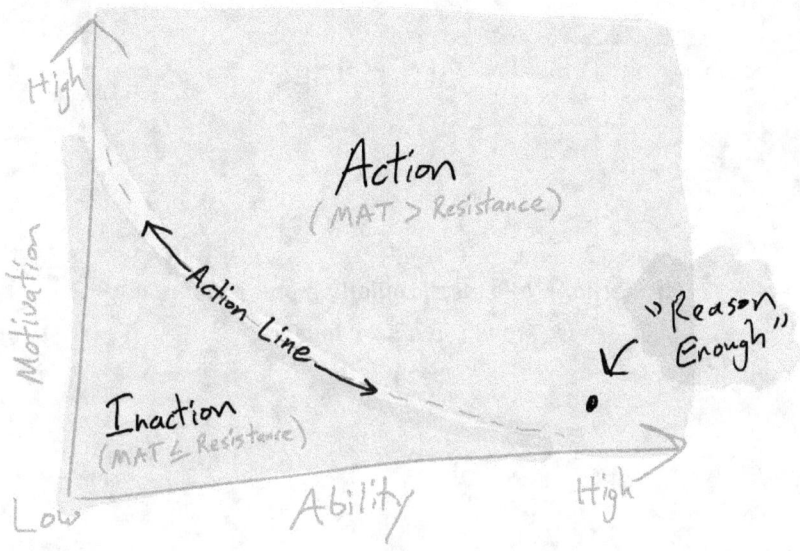

When your ability is high, motivation doesn't matter. To do what you *should* be doing, all you need is **"reason enough."**

Assuming you don't miss your triggers...

44

The 3rd Bridge

"My mechanic told me, 'I couldn't repair your brakes,
so I made your horn louder.'"
-Steven Wright

- You made it to the gym, but forgot your gym bag.
- You went to the restaurant, but forgot to ask for a to-go box.
- You meant to go to bed, but didn't set an alarm.

Even when motivation and ability are high, you can fail to TRIGGER the right behaviors.

And when you miss them...

Crickets.

Nothing happens.

But this shouldn't happen...

Triggers are EVERYWHERE.

Your senses are looking for them, conscious or not, 24/7/365.

Put the right triggers, in the right places, at the right times and:

- You make fewer mistakes
- You make better choices
- You become more consistent

No more:

- Forgetting your gym bag at home
- Forgetting to your to-go box

- Getting to bed too late

Or other well laid plans that never get put into practice.

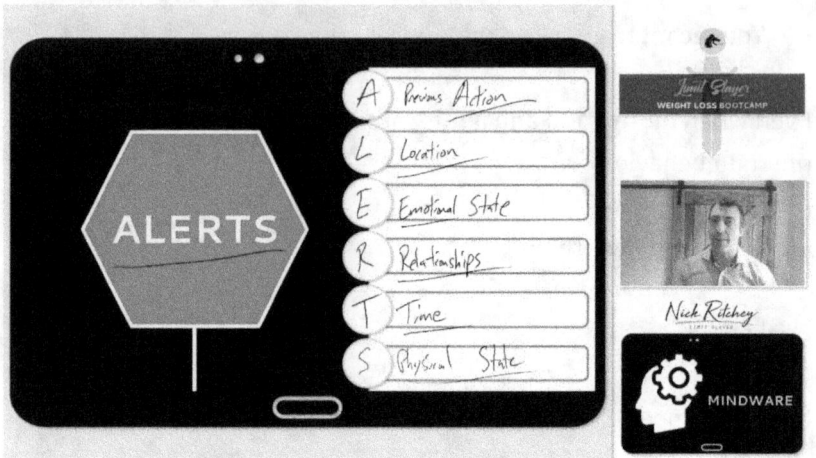

You can remember your triggers with "A.L.E.R.T.S."

- (A)ctivity (current or preceding)
- (L)ocation (or environmental factor)
- (E)motion
- (R)elationship
- (T)ime
- (S)tate (physical)

You can use one or more of these triggers to activate the right concepts, mindsets and actions as you need them.

Here are some examples.

Pretend you have the hardest time remembering to put your gym bag into the car. Here's how you can use A.L.E.R.T.S. to stop forgetting.

A - ACTIVITY

What ACTIVITY precedes putting your gym bag into the car?

If you brush your teeth before heading out the door, you could:

- Put a reminder on your bathroom mirror
- Leave your gym bag on the bathroom counter
- Keep your toothbrush in your gym bag

These tie your desired behavior (gym bag into car) with the preceding activity (brushing your teeth).

L - LOCATION

What LOCATION triggers putting your gym bag into the car?

After brushing your teeth, you could take your gym bag from the bathroom counter and throw it in front of your door. To leave the house, you'll need to pick it up.

E - EMOTION

What EMOTION triggers putting your gym bag into the car?

Are you rushed in the morning and scrambling to get out of the house?

If so, create some mindware to associate these feelings with a desire to put your gym bag in your car.

R - RELATIONSHIP

What RELATIONSHIP triggers putting your gym bag into the car?

If you get a kiss from your loving partner in the morning before heading out the door, why not make it 2?! Enlist their help! Get that first kiss, check for your gym bag together... and one more before heading out the door! (gym bag in hand)

T - TIME

What TIME triggers putting your gym bag into the car?

If you leave the house at 8 every morning, set an alarm on your phone for 7:58 to remind you to pick up your gym bag.

S - STATE

What physical STATE triggers putting your gym bag in the car?

- Hands feel a bit lighter than they should?
- Jittery from coffee but not rattling your gym bag?

Use this physical state to trigger a gym bag check.

With practice you'll discover:

- Some A.L.E.R.T.S. work better than others
- The more A.L.E.R.T.S., the merrier
- Physical A.L.E.R.T.S. often trump mental ones

By "making your horn louder" you stop forgetting & start remembering...

Unless you "have a terrible memory."

45

The 4th Bridge

"Neurons that fire together, wire together."
–Donald Hebb

Imagine going through bootcamp, and discovering people who keep food logs:

- Lose twice as much weight as dieters who don't
- In minutes a day
- Which, compared to cardio, is 20-60x more efficient

You think, "Wow, I should start a food log!"

But after a good night's sleep, you forget all about it.

Until you encounter it again...

YEARS later.

You're slogging away on the treadmill. Come across the power of food logs... again. And think to yourself, "With all the time I've spent on this machine, why haven't I tried food logging yet?!"

Because <u>forgetting is normal.</u>

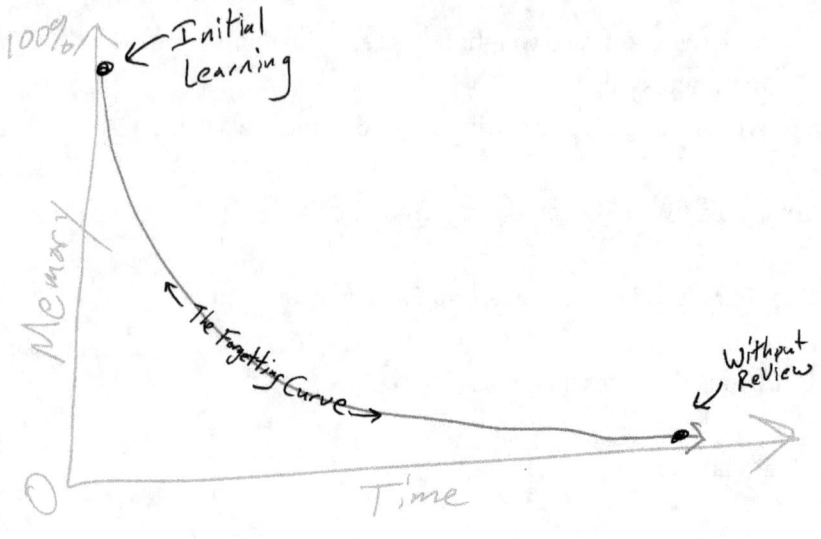

The Ebbinghaus forgetting curve (above) shows how we forget most things without review. But when you add distributed practice into the mix, it changes:

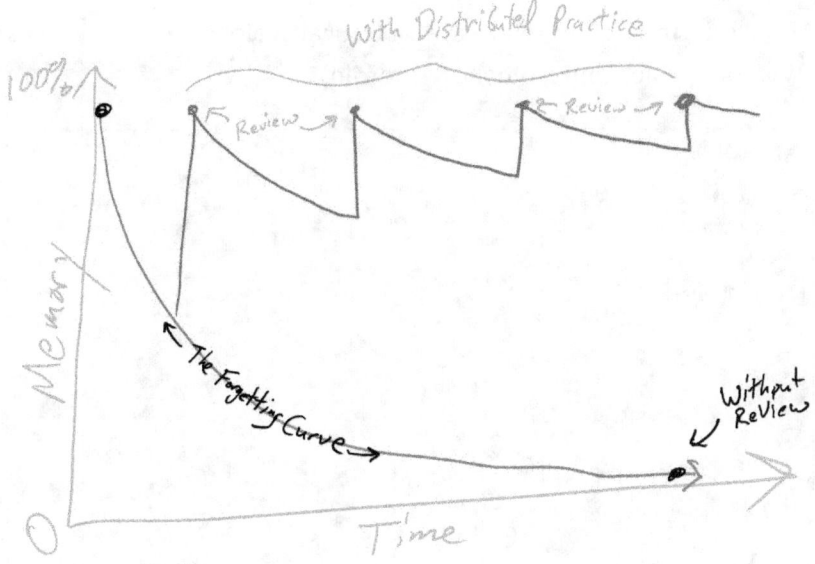

Forgetting becomes a choice.

You can remember anything you want.

You just need:

- A good reason
- The right tools

Here are the basics:

- Put what you want to remember on digital flash cards
- Include the A.L.E.R.T.S. to trigger them under the right conditions
- Start reviewing them with spaced repetition software

My favorite program is ANKI - available for all major operating systems (Windows, Mac, Linux, iPhone & Android).

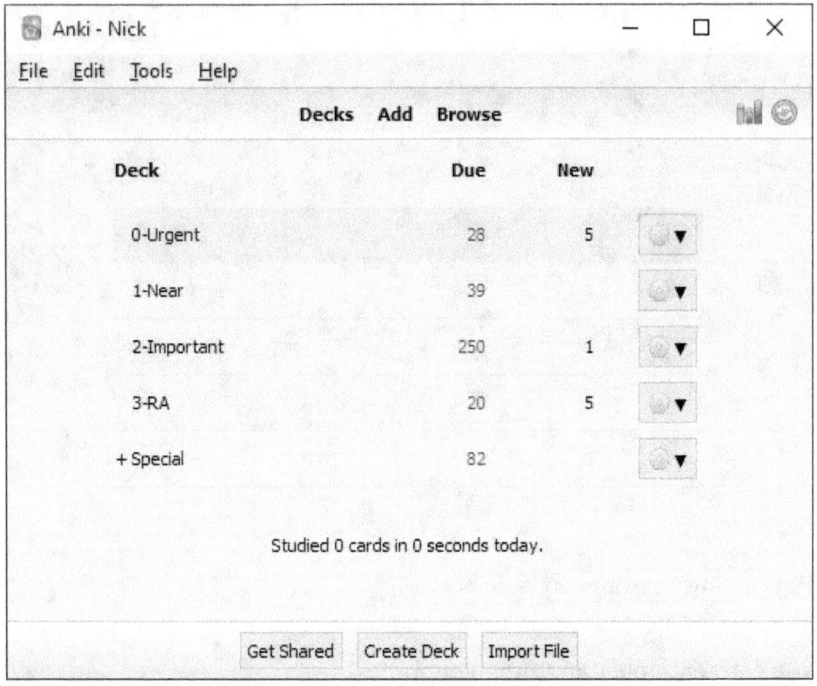

Nick's ANKI at the start of a new day.

The next time you open your phone to:

- Check e-mail
- Check Facebook
- Watch Netflix
- Etc.

Open your flash card software FIRST.

Spend a few minutes reviewing the concepts, mindsets & actions which will transform your life and body. Then continue whatever your were doing.

You can fix & maintain all 4 bridges (R.A.T.S.) with:

- Well-constructed mindware
- A few minutes of daily practice

That's all it takes...

MINUTES a day.

And these minutes prevent hours (sometimes YEARS) of mistakes.

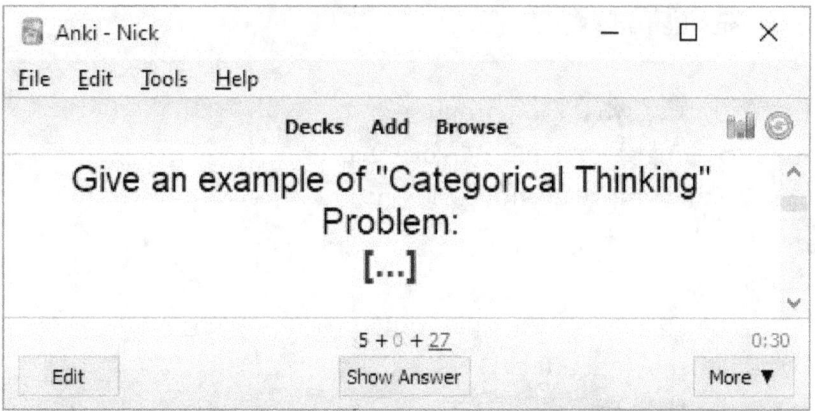

Random example – this cue prompts Nick to generate examples of "categorical thinking" problems. This review leads to better awareness, monitoring & remembering.

If you suffer from a "terrible" memory, you're not alone.

Many polyglots, polymaths, memory champions and other "geniuses" start with "poor" memories. But they use spaced repetition and other techniques to improve their SKILLS.

And discover they can remember more than the UNSKILLED masses.

This helps them think:

· Faster
· Easier
· More efficiently

This leads to thinking more EFFECTIVELY. And turns ordinary Janes & Joes into "practical geniuses."

Because when you STOP:

· Forgetting what's important
· Repeating painful mistakes over & over
· Wasting time reinventing the wheel

And START:

· Doing the right things
· At the right times
· In the right ways

You gain an "unfair" advantage.

Improving your memory doesn't just make you a leaner person…

It makes you a better person.

46

Beyond Stagnation

"All life is problem solving."
-Karl Popper

Breaking through your plateaus, one by one, gets you to Milestone 5: Evolution.

Where you become a weight loss BlackBelt.

Where you:

- Have the body you've always wanted
- Stay lean easily & automatically

And NEVER have to worry about your weight EVER again.

You've learned the root cause of most stagnation lies in false concepts, fixed mindsets & flawed actions. When the roots are healthy, you need to check your bridges for R.A.T.S...

- Failure to (R)emember
- Failure to (A)ctivate
- Failure to (T)rigger
- Failure to (S)tore...

The right concepts/mindsets/actions at the right times (under the right conditions).

When things go wrong, it's not the end of the world.

Because you're going to learn from the **pain**, and turn it into **power**.

You already know WHAT concepts, mindsets & actions you need.

Now we're going to look at HOW to put them into practice in a way that makes most of this chapter IRRELEVANT.

No, you didn't waste your time.

And yes, our goal is to PREVENT most of these problems before they happen.

Wouldn't it be nice if you could avoid stagnation altogether?

When you IMPROVE in the right way, you can...

47

Milestone 3: Improvement

*"Nothing builds self-esteem and self-confidence
like accomplishment."*
-Thomas Carlyle

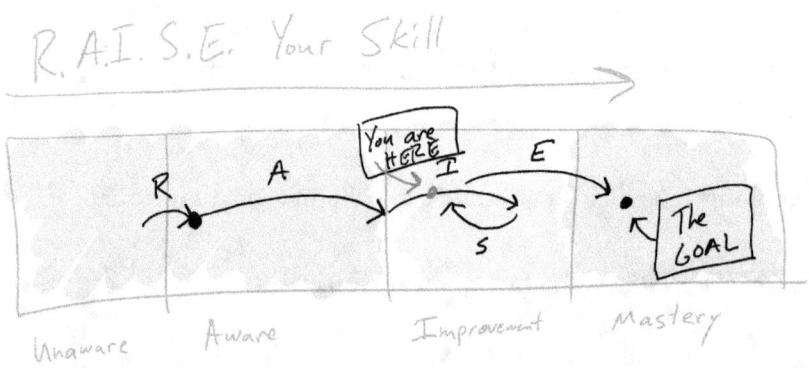

Yes, we just covered milestone 4 (stagnation) and are now covering milestone 3 (improvement). It's a bit backwards, but not without reason.

Now that you understand where problems come from, preventing them will make more sense.

So let's back up and pretend you've gone through the first 2 legs of the journey:

- You realized you need to lose weight
- And you've started improving your S.T.A.N.D.ing

As a result...

You're losing weight & feeling great.

The actions you're taking are finally paying off. Despite looking & feeling better than you have in years, you wish things were a little easier...

AND more enjoyable.

Don't worry.

We're going to make getting to weight loss baseline:

- Easier to achieve
- More enjoyable
- More engaging
- More meaningful

AND give you better results in the process.

Let's have some FUN!

48

Triple the Fun (TRR)

I tell my clients, *"Enjoy succeeding where others suffer to fail."*

And it's one of the most POWERFUL mindsets you can adopt.

- Some people DREAD going to the gym, while others look forward to it.
- Some people HATE their workouts, while others LOVE them.
- Some people feel DRAINED after working out, others feel ENER-GIZED.

What's the difference?

The difference lies in how much we enjoy each part of the feedback loop. This is what Charles Duhigg calls a "habit loop" in his book, "The Power of Habit."

Feedback loops take the form:

(T)rigger → (R)esponse → (R)eward

Here is how they fit into our behavior model:

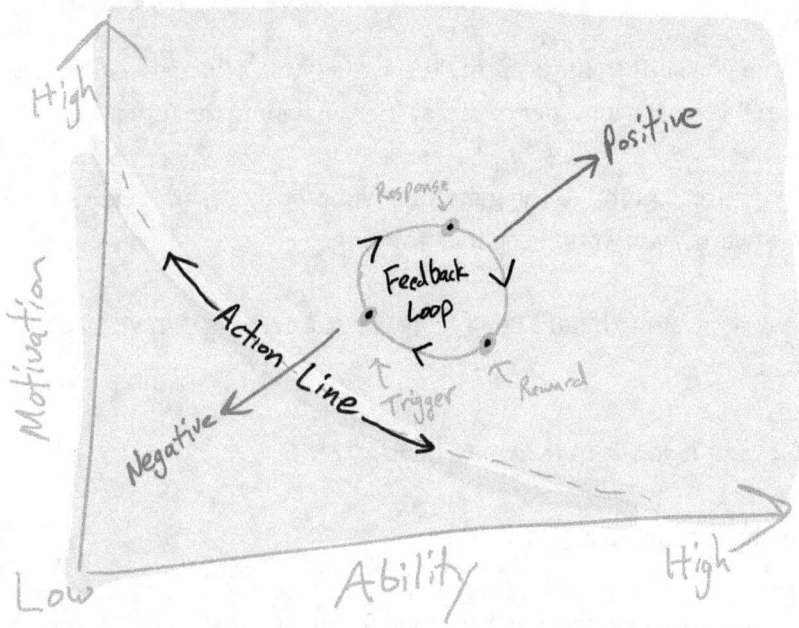

As you can see, your feedback loop can affect future behavior:

· It can stay in the same place
· Shift up/right
· Shift down/left

When you shift up/right, we call this a "positive feedback loop." It makes the behavior self-reinforcing.

An example is where you look forward to going to the gym, enjoy your workout, and feel great afterwards.

You can't wait to go back.

This is a positive feedback loop. Create these for the skills you need to master, and getting lean becomes fun!

When you shift to the bottom-left, we call this a "negative feedback loop." It makes it harder to repeat the behavior in the future.

If you dread going to the gym, hate your workout, and feel terrible afterwards, you won't keep it up for long.

So if you want to build a habit, you want to create POSITIVE feedback loops.

But what if you want to break a habit?

You have 2 options:

1. Create a negative feedback loop for the habit
2. Create a positive feedback loop for a substitute (better) habit

And MOST people choose wrong...

They punish themselves for their mistakes, hoping it will prevent them from screwing up in the future. The only problem is...

It doesn't work most of the time.

From addiction research, we know **substitution** tends to work better.

For example, how much guilt have you felt about over-eating in the past?

And how much did it prevent over-eating in the future?

Not much, right?

So you only need to learn about POSITIVE feedback loops for now.

To make improving easier & more rewarding:

- Identify your bad habits
- Find better ones to replace them
- Reinforce the new habits with positive feedback loops

You have 3 opportunities to make your feedback loops positive:

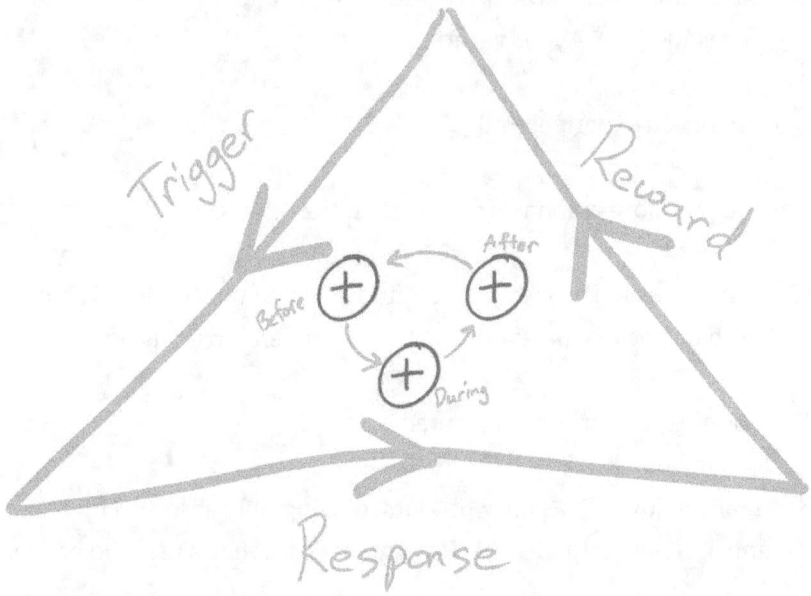

You can reinforce your new habits:

- Before doing them *(Trigger)*
- While doing them *(Response)*
- After doing them *(Reward)*

You're probably good at one of these naturally because of something known as a temporal bias. That is, you tend to focus on one of these 3 time frames more than the others.

Pretend you're going on vacation.

Would you describe yourself as someone who:

- Loves PLANNING the vacation (future anticipation)
- Loves BEING on vacation (present mindfulness)
- Loves RELIVING your vacation (past savoring)

Of course, you experience all 3.

But you put more emphasis on one than the others.

When it comes to the gym, IF you find a way to make it enjoyable, it will probably be in whatever time frame you tend to focus on.

For example, I'm present-oriented.

So I really enjoy DOING my workouts. Getting fully absorbed in lifting weights that will cripple me if I'm not careful... that's my kind of fun!

But I don't naturally look forward to going to the gym, or want to spend time savoring my accomplishments.

"Who cares if yesterday was the best day of my life?!...
  I want to feel good NOW!"

That's how my mind works when left to its own devices.

So I have to remind myself...

If I just get my ass into the gym, I'm going to have a great time (future anticipation).

And some days, you'll feel sluggish and weak in the gym. Remember all the great progress you've made (savoring past accomplishments).

By making all 3 time frames rewarding, you're making it easier to succeed.

And harder to fail.

You can visualize it like this:

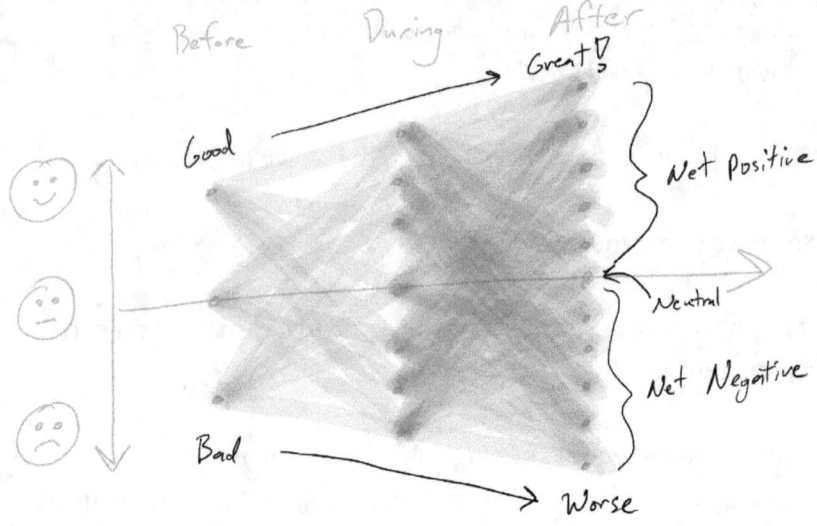

At any stage of the experience, things can get better or worse.

But getting off to a good start makes it easier to have a positive experience.

You create the strongest positive feedback loop when you:

- Look forward to your activity
- Enjoy it
- Feel great about it afterwards

For example...

To create a positive feedback loop for the gym, you need:

1. A workout you love
2. Some kind of reward at the end

3. And to think about the reward at the start

Making positive post-workout experiences is easy. Make a plan to reward yourself, and stick to it. It doesn't have to be big, expensive or fancy.

Think simple pleasures.

A cup of hand-ground coffee. A few minutes with a silly book or video game. Any little guilty pleasure is fine... as long as it doesn't sabotage your weight loss (e.g. junk food as a reward for working out is a big no-no).

And don't skimp out.

You promised yourself a reward...

AND you earned it...

So enjoy it!

For positive pre-workout experiences :

1. Make sure there's a reward waiting for you at the end
2. Log your peak positive experiences in & after the gym
3. Set goals & record your progress as you make it
4. Throw these into your mindware for review

You're using immediate (post-workout) and variable rewards (chance to create new memories & progress). And this combination should have you salivating to go to the gym like a Pavlovian dog in no time.

As for the peri-workout experience itself, let's make it P.E.R.M.A.nent...

49

Make it P.E.R.M.A.nent

"Wondrous is the strength of cheerfulness, and its power of endurance - the cheerful man will do more in the same time, will do it better, will preserve it longer, than the sad or sullen."
-Thomas Carlyle

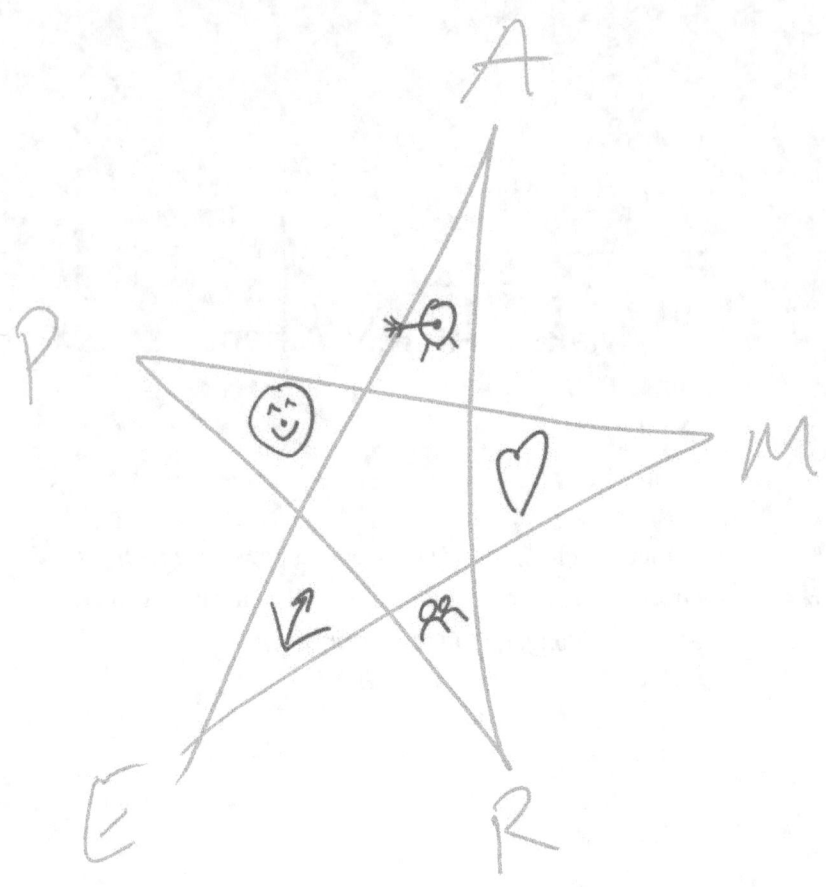

P.E.R.M.A. stands for:

- (P)ositive Emotions
- (E)ngagement
- (R)elationships
- (M)eaning
- (A)chievement

These are the 5 pillars of happiness taught by Martin Seligman (one of the founding fathers of positive psychology). I was lucky to learn about them from Marty himself back when there were 4 pillars…

And I've been using them ever since.

Now YOU can use P.E.R.M.A. to make any skill you're mastering more enjoyable.

All you need to do is ask and answer a few simple questions…

Pretend one day, you're getting in your 15 minutes of NEPA. You're on a treadmill, staring at the wall…

And bored to TEARS!

That's when you remember to ask yourself a P.E.R.M.A. question…

"What would NEPA look like if I were having a wildly good time, full of positive emotions, during my NEPA?"

Here are some things my clients enjoy more than slogging away on the treadmill:

- Zumba classes
- Ping pong
- Gardening
- Biking outdoors
- Buying a dog (and walking it!)

Let's pretend you switch to Zumba.

So you start getting more NEPA, more easily because you're having more fun.

It's an improvement.

But not enough to impress Marty...

So let's make your new NEPA even MORE enjoyable.

The next question is,

"How can I make Zumba even more engaging?"

Our local community center offers several Zumba classes. And my wife was sorely disappointed with the first.

Better than nothing, but it was TOO EASY!

So remembering FLOW, she tried another class.

It was harder, and more fun because it matched her skill level.

The next question is,

"How can I improve relationships in my Zumba class?"

Maybe you:

- Get some friends to join you
- Make new friends through class
- Get to know the instructor

- Bring in some low-cal treats once a month

It's up to you.

Just connect & have fun!

For my wife, of course, this meant getting ME to join. I was reluctant at first, but she was having so much fun, I decided to give it a try.

Now I'm hooked.

It's not something I'd do on my own, but together, it's a good time.

In the words of Christopher Peterson (another founder of positive psychology),

"Other people matter."

Now, instead of staring at a wall, walking alone on a treadmill...

- You're grooving to the music
- Getting into flow
- Having fun with friends

And experiencing what Barbara Fredrickson calls the "broaden and build" effect. All these positive emotions help you become more creative, flexible and spontaneous.

Which tend to lead to lasting physical, mental and social benefits.

And you can make your NEPA even more P.E.R.M.A.nent by infusing it with meaning and achievement.

Remember WHY weight loss was so important to you in the first place, and HOW it's going to transform your life.

Isn't it wonderful that your new Zumba class isn't just fun and rewarding by itself, but also helps you get leaner?

How cool is that!

For achievement:

- Create a goal (search "S.M.A.R.T.E.R. Goals" for bonus points)
- Show up
- Track progress

Seeing progress over time is its own form of reward.

When you achieve your goals, carve out some TIME and SPACE to celebrate them.

You can infuse ANYTHING with P.E.R.M.A.

And like FLOW, once you "get it," you're hooked.

The more P.E.R.M.A., the merrier.

If you want to enjoy getting & staying lean for life...

Make your S.T.A.N.D.ing P.E.R.M.A.nent!

50

"Sprint" for Faster Results

"Every obstacle yields to stern resolve."
–Leonardo Da Vinci

"Hey Nick, isn't there ANY way to speed things up?!"

Of course, there are MANY ways to speed things up. You can:

- Identify your weight loss limiter
- Spend more time improving your skills
- Increase the frequency of skill practice
- And...

"No. No. No... I mean, yeah. All that. But something, you know, a bit more challenging?"

Our primary focus in this book is making your weight loss S.A.F.E. & Simple. Because improving your PERMA S.T.A.N.D.ing is the fastest way I know to make & keep you lean for life.

And the journey is more like a marathon than a sprint.

The LENGTH of the race doesn't change. But the time and energy you spend getting to the finish line can vary depending on your approach.

Your current toolbox includes:

- S.T.A.N.D.ing still (not regressing)
- Walking (Engineering for Success)
- Jogging (S.T.A.N.D.ing up)
- Sprinting (Special Challenges)

When you have some extra energy, you're free to kick into high gear for a while. And it'll bring you to the finish line a little faster.

As long as you don't overdo it.

"Sprints" are NOT sustainable (for the most part).

But they can help you get the scale moving while you wait for the delayed response of your habits to catch-up.

Here's an example which you shouldn't try until:

- You've cleared it with your physician
- Your training S.T.A.N.D.ing is GREEN

This means most readers SHOULD NOT try it now.

But if you meet the criteria, and like the idea, feel free to give it a go! If you do give it a shot, send an e-mail to:

Nick@LimitSlayer.com

And tell me how it went!

GT (Green Training) Challenge: "No Dice"

- Material needed: 1 dice
- Difficulty: (4-8)/10 (depending on your luck & tolerance)

Question: "Why must I be GREEN with TRAINING?"

Because without training, you risk losing muscle mass. Ultimately, with less muscle, you'll make ALL future fat loss HARDER than it needs to be.

Step 1: Challenge Duration

Roll the dice until you get a 1, 2 or 3.

This is the number of weeks you will stick with the challenge.

Step 2: Fasting Duration

If today's a training day, you don't roll the dice.

No dice on training day.

If today is an off day (non-training), you roll the dice. Again, re-roll until you get a 1,2 or 3. This is how many meals you're going to skip.

I'm assuming you eat 3 meals a day. If you eat more or less, adjust the dice accordingly.

Here's an example.

Step 1: You roll a 6.

This is not a 1,2, or 3, so you re-roll the dice. You roll a 2. This means you're going to stick to the challenge for 2 weeks.

Step 2: On your off day, you roll a 4. Re-roll. You roll a 1. This means you get to skip breakfast (B), lunch (L) or dinner (D).

It's up to you.

Special Exception #1

If you have less than 20lbs to lose, don't skip more than 6 meals a week. Instead, add X0 minutes of NEPA (where X is the number on the die).

For example, if you only have 15lbs left to your weight loss goal, have fasted 6 meals already this week, and roll a 3, you:

Do 30 minutes (X0 become 30) of extra NEPA instead of fasting

Special Exception #2

If you're not training frequently, and supposed to fast more than 6 consecutive meals in a row, use the NEPA rule above instead.

Progression

If you're never fasted before, I recommend the following progression.

When you roll the dice on the first day, treat all numbers as a "1."

You get to skip 1 meal.

Once you get the "OK" from your doc, you realize skipping one meal isn't a big deal.

This is **"intermittent fasting."**

You don't need to read a 300 page book to understand how skipping 1 meal decreases EI (energy in).

When you're ready for more of a challenge, you can switch to even/odd rolls.

- Roll an odd number, you skip 1 meal
- Roll an even number, you skip 2 meals

A 2-meal fast is often referred to as a "4-hour" eating window, or "The Warrior Diet." It's a longer intermittent fast.

Again, no need for a 300 page book.

It's 2 meals without food.

Less EI.

This isn't rocket science, but you wouldn't know it from the books on the shelf...

NEXT!

Once you start feeling comfortable with 2-meal fasts, you can start doing full day fasts when you roll a 3.

Here's where things get a little interesting.

If you have several non-training days in a row, you may end up doing multi-day fasts (e.g. Rolling 3, 3).

This might sound INSANE if you've never fasted before.

But if you follow the progression & exceptions, you'll find:

- The more weight you have to lose, the easier it is
- It'll get you lean about as fast as naturally possible

TIP #1: Do this with a friend / housemate.

Remember the "R" in PERMA?

This, like most challenges, is more fun with friends.

Do step 1 together, so you're both locked into it. Then roll your days individually. When you're unlucky, talk to your friend. When they're unlucky, they can talk to you.

Offer support, encouragement, and have fun!

TIP #2: Chain Your Meals

Let's pretend you have 3 days off in a row from training.

Roll all 3 days in advance to make a chain.

Pretend your dice rolls are 1,3,2.

Your fasting could look like this:

- Day 1: skip B, eat LD
- Day 2: skip BLD
- Day 3: eat B, skip LD

You get food on days 1 & 3, but you're doing 3 fasts around them. And most people find the first 1-2 meals are the hardest to skip.

So you're struggling more than you need to.

By chaining the fasts together, it looks like this:

- Day 1: eat BL, skip D
- Day 2: skip BLD

- Day 3: skip BL, eat D

Here, you only go through 1 tough start, and you fast until you're done.

You'll probably find chaining easier than frequent starts & stops.

PLUS, you remove the chance of going terribly wrong (overeating) during the meals in the middle.

Frequently Asked Questions

"What kind of fast are we talking about?"

This is a water-only fast. Continue to drink water as usual, but no food or drinks other than water.

"Isn't fasting dangerous?"

Whatever your doc says, that's your answer.

When I was 80lbs overweight, I asked my doc about fasting. He said it was probably a good idea since my weight was obviously impacting my health. And added that 1 day a week without food shouldn't hurt me.

Now, we're only going 2 days in a row MAX on this protocol.

No big deal if you have the medical clearance.

Seneca advises,

"Endure all this for three or four days at a time, sometimes for more, so that it may be a test of yourself instead of a mere hobby. Then, I assure you, my dear Lucilius, you will leap for joy when filled with a pennyworth of food, and you will understand that a man's peace of mind does not depend upon Fortune."

I've fasted 7 days out of curiosity.

30-40 days fasts were not uncommon in ancient religions. And you'll find YouTubers all over the place doing 30-day fasts.

This isn't to say I recommend extreme fasting...

FAR FROM IT!

In fact, long-term:

- I don't recommend intermittent fasting
- I don't recommend alternate-day-fasting
- I don't recommend multi-day fasts

Simply because you won't need it.

Done right, you don't need fasting to stay lean.

It's only there to speed up the process. Fasting is one of many tools in your weight loss toolbox. Use it to speed up weight loss for a short time.

Then return to an easier pace.

"What about dry fasting?"

This is an example of chasing diminishing returns. If you're experienced with water fasting, feel free to talk to your doc. Otherwise, start with water fasts.

Walk before you run.

"Can I do demanding physical activity during a fast?"

No. This is why we don't fast on training days. You're more likely to get light-headed, and this can lead to injury. I break this rule regularly, but only because my body can tolerate it.

Other people pass out and get hurt.

You should be fine with light-moderate activity, but avoid high-intensity activities. Again, walk before you run.

"How do I break a longer fast?"

2 days shouldn't cause any problems. But if you have digestive issues, keep the first meal small-medium sized made of gentle, real food.

For example, consider:

- Popcorn + fake butter + greasy nachos + 2 hoppy beers
- VS. a small plate of mild meat, potatoes and veggies...

The first may turn your stomach upside down...

The second should be fine.

"Why no more than 6 consecutive meals?"

If your nutrition and training are really dialed in, 3 days is about the max you can go without losing unnecessary muscle mass. Also, after 3 days, your body starts becoming protective of its fat stores.

This causes diminishing returns.

The work isn't worth the payoff.

A 2-day MAX gives you all the benefits without the drawbacks.

"Why dice?"

2 Reasons...

1. Dice are less psychologically taxing.

We're removing your thinking/choosing from the equation. Instead of it being YOUR fault for missing 2 days of food, it's the dice's fault.

PLUS, when you roll a small number, you breathe a sigh of relief. You're still moving in the right direction — FASTER than normal. But it's a short sprint.

2. Dice are fun!

While teaching math, I recognized students who helped others, participated, and put in a good effort. And to make the most of it, I used dice.

Dice are a "variable reward" (Thanks B.F. Skinner!) which helped me have fun, save a ton of cash, and increase participation (more than consistent rewards).

So when students did something well in my class, they got rewarded twice. Once with a roll of the dice (anticipation), and once with the prize dictated by the dice roll.

The most coveted reward was the candy bar (roll a 12).

The 2nd was 2 mini-candy bars (roll snake eyes).

And the other 9 ranged from high-fives, to writing a special message on the board, to changing seats... I wish my teachers had used dice in math class (and weight loss)!

"When should I do sprints?"

This is up to you, but most people do them:

- After vacation
- When you're getting impatient
- When you're stuck on a plateau

I like to fully enjoy my vacations...

That's the point, right?! But because of this, I always gain 5-10lbs. Before I got to weight loss baseline, it used to be 30-40!

To counterbalance being "a lot worse than usual" for a short time, you need to be "a little better than usual" for a long time.

As William James said earlier, it's like carefully rolling up a ball of string... then dropping it. You can undo your weight loss a lot faster than you can redo it.

This is why improving your weight loss baseline is so important.

You encounter milder setbacks, less often. And make better progress, for longer periods.

By the time you get to vacation, the setback is no big deal.

You enjoy yourself, gain a couple pounds.

And then they come off.

No big deal.

"Are there other challenges?"

You bet! But not in this book.

In my coaching program we have challenges based on your current

S.T.A.N.D.ing.

Have all red (AR) lights?
    Try the AR challenge.

Just got to green in diet (GD)?
    Try the GD Challenge

Just got to yellow in sleep (YS)?
    Try the YS challenge

Challenges are fun, motivating, and get you the results you're after, faster.

If you decide to join us, every time you improve your S.T.A.N.D.ing, you have a new challenge to look forward to.

51

M.A.T.R.R.s of Habit

"Habit is ten times nature."
–Duke of Wellington

We're almost at the end of the book, so this is where it all starts coming together.

To get to weight loss baseline, you need to master the 5 basic skills (STAND). And to become a master, you need time, improvement & consistency (TIC).

To be consistent, you need to:

- Show up
- And do the work
- In a way which is self-reinforcing

Recall "showing up and doing the work" depends on:

B=MAT *(Motivation, Ability, Trigger)*

And self-reinforcing feedback loops take the form:

T → R → R *(Trigger, Response, Reward)*

And what are habits?

They're behaviors repeated consistently over time.

Habit = behavior (MAT) repeated (TRR)
   = MAT * TRR
   = MATRR (no double counting of triggers)

Mastery is a M.A.T.R.R. of improving habits.

So becoming a weight loss BlackBelt is just a M.A.T.R.R. of making the right habits.

You've seen this before:

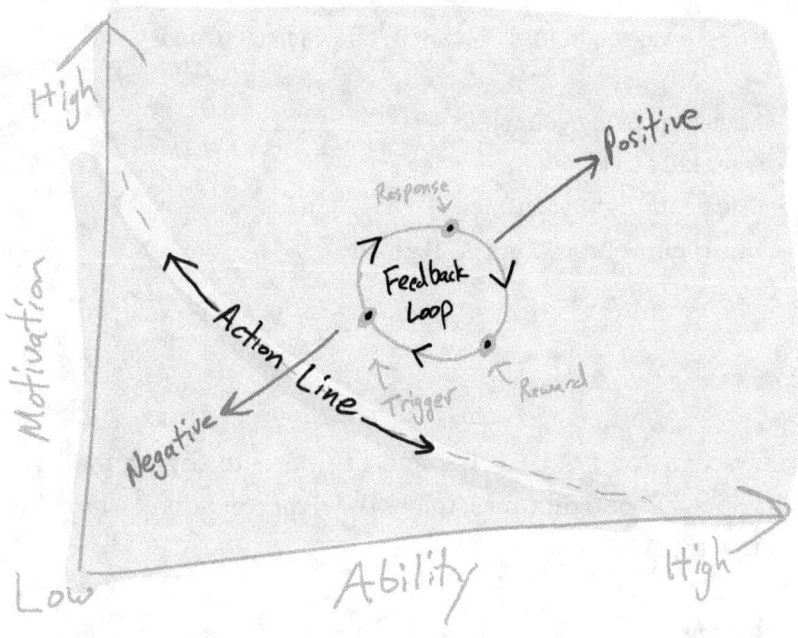

The magic is in the process...

Motivation

Harness motivation when you have it. Because it makes everything easier. But because motivation wanes, you can't rely on it. You get around this by matching your challenges to your current skill level.

When you do, you experience flow.

This makes motivation a happy bonus rather than a necessity.

Ability

To get 80% to weight loss BlackBelt, all you need to do is:

- Keep improving your skills
- One skill at a time
- One traffic light at a time
- Until your S.T.A.N.D.ing is all green

Trigger

Be aware of the 5 A.L.E.R.T.S. and use them to trigger the right behaviors, at the right times, under the right conditions. Start with external triggers:

- Alarms
- Physical engineering
- Phone / calendar reminders
- Etc.

And progress to internal triggers (mindware mastery).

Response

To make your improvement more enjoyable and lasting...

Infuse your skill building with P.E.R.M.A.

And don't forget to optimize for flow!

Reward

The long-term reward is the body & life you create.

But short-term, you want something to look forward to IMMEDI-ATELY.

You can reward yourself 3 times:

- Before (anticipation)
- During (P.E.R.M.A.-flow with your strengths)
- After (small, immediate treat)

For example, after writing each chapter of this book I get to:

- Play outside for 10 minutes
- Brew a fresh cup of half-caff coffee
- Play 5 minutes of video games

This rewards me in 3 ways:

- Anticipating fresh air, caffeine, fun and progress
- Having fun helping others using my strengths
- Savoring progress and celebrating after a job well done

Mastery is just a M.A.T.R.R. of improving habits.

If your weight loss baseline habits get you 80% of the way there...

What about the other 20%?

52

Control the M.O.B.S.

*"The only defense that is more than pretense
is to act on the fact that there is no defense."*
-Piet Hein

The other 20% of weight loss is all about how you deal with problems.

We covered this when looking at Milestone 4: Stagnation.

But here's a helpful tip on WHAT to work on first if you're taking a DIY (do-it-yourself) approach. This is the same process I use to help PRIORITIZE what my clients work on next.

First, you number out everything in your problem log.

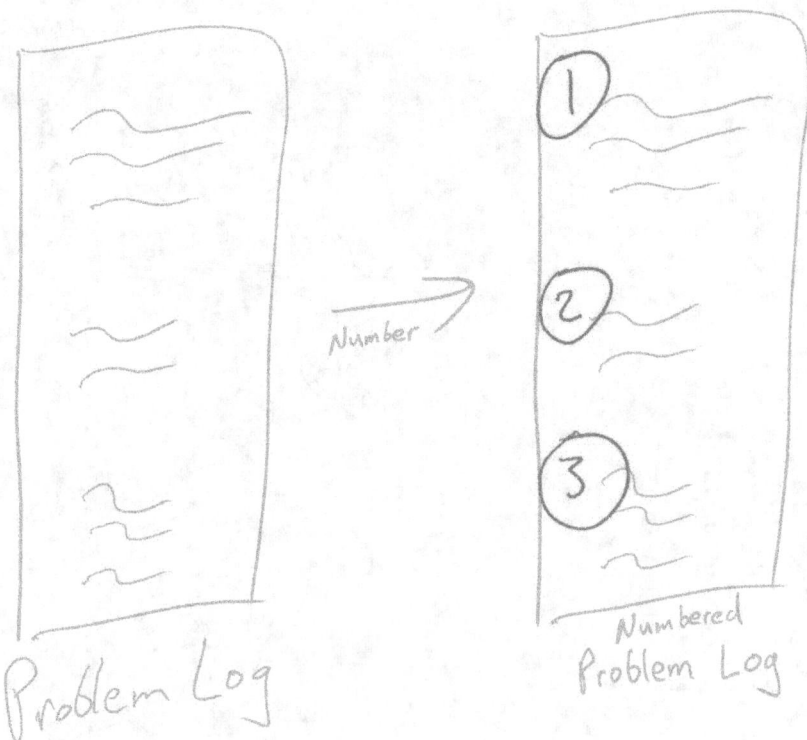

The second step is to "Control the M.O.B.S." by plotting them on the matrix:

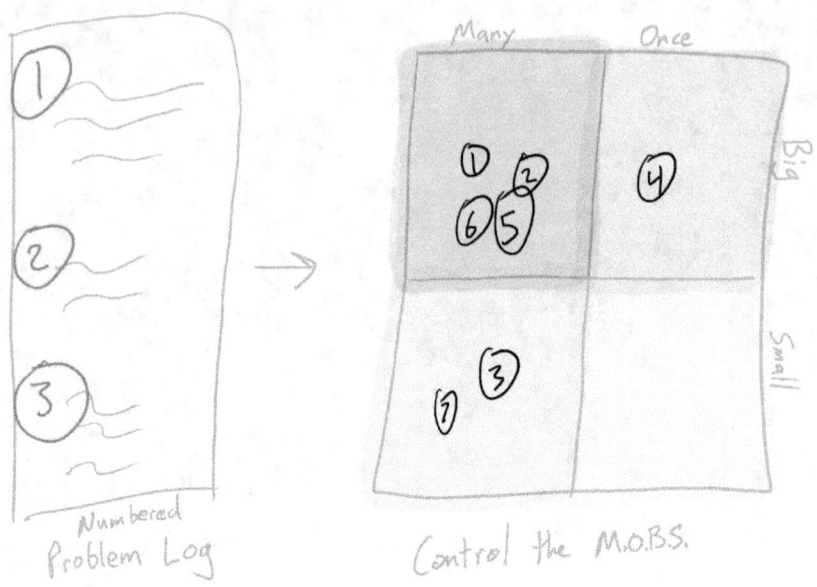

M.O.B.S. stands for:

- Many – it's a recurring problem
- Once – if it only happens once (or infrequently)
- Big – it's a big problem
- Small – it's a small problem

Once you've plotted your problems, look at what to solve first in terms of ease & impact. You can do this with your entire problem log, or parts of it.

Let's pretend you have a long list of problems, so you focus on clearing out the MB quadrant first (these are your big, recurring problems):

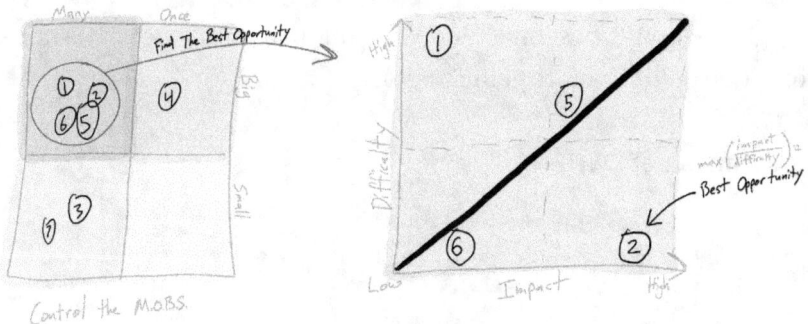

Control the M.O.B.S.

In the graph above, everything below the diagonal line (dividing red from green) is well worth the effort. In this case, 6 and 2 are well worth the effort...

Because the impact outweighs the difficulty.

The BEST opportunity is #2 because it will be easy to solve and have a BIG impact. Since this is a recurring problem, once you solve it, you won't have to worry about it EVER AGAIN...

Your life will be PERMANENTLY better.

In this way, one problem at a time, you turn **pain** into **power**.

If you take a DIY approach, I recommend reading:

- "Problem Solving 101" by Ken Watanabe
- "Principles" by Ray Dalio

And if you join us, look forward to an entire week of bootcamp devoted to this process. We go into more depth. And break it down in detail, step-by-step.

By getting to WL baseline & looping your pain into power, it's not a question of "IF" you're going to get lean...

It's a matter of "WHEN."

53

Summary

"So far as we are thus mere bundles of habit, we are stereotyped creatures, imitators and copiers of our past selves. And since this, under any circumstances, is what we always tend to become, it follows first of all that the teacher's prime concern should be to ingrain into the pupil that assortment of habits that shall be most useful to him throughout life. Education is for behavior, and habits are the stuff of which behavior consists."

-William James

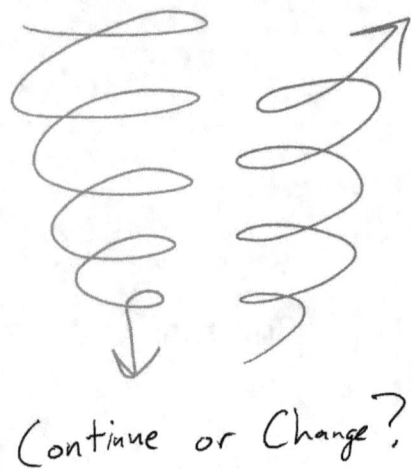

Continue or Change?

It's been a long journey...

But you made it to the end of the book!

You now understand what most people don't...

Weight loss is a SKILL.

As such, it goes through 4 stages of development:

Those who stop at conscious competence, LOSE.

They work hard for the rest of their lives to stay lean. And usually gain the weight back before they die.

There is only one "true" form of weight loss success.

Mastery.

"Unconscious competence" gets you lean for life...

Nothing else.

And all mastery passes 5 milestones:

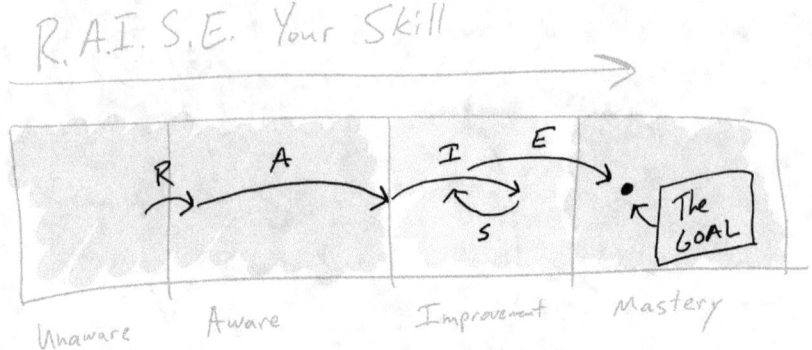

1. (R)ealization
2. (A)ction
3. (I)mprovement
4. (S)tagnation
5. (E)volution

With a lot of bouncing between improvement and stagnation until you get to mastery.

To get off on the right foot, you want to make your weight loss S.A.F.E. & Simple:

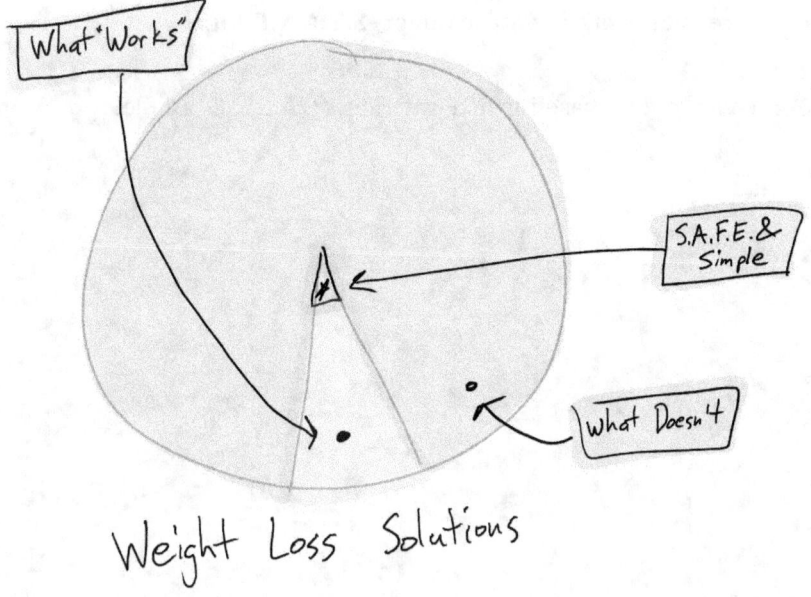

Weight Loss Solutions

Because if it's not (S)ustainable, the results won't last.

If it's not (A)utomatic, you're forced to think (and forget) for a lifetime.

If it's not (F)lexible, your quality of life will suck.

If it's not (E)asy, you'll struggle until the day you tire of struggling.

And if it's not (S)imple, you won't act.

And despite the MASSIVE amount of information in this book...

Weight loss IS simple.

It boils down to this...

If you're over-weight, you're under-S.T.A.N.D.ing.

Get to weight loss baseline in a way that's S.A.F.E. & Simple:

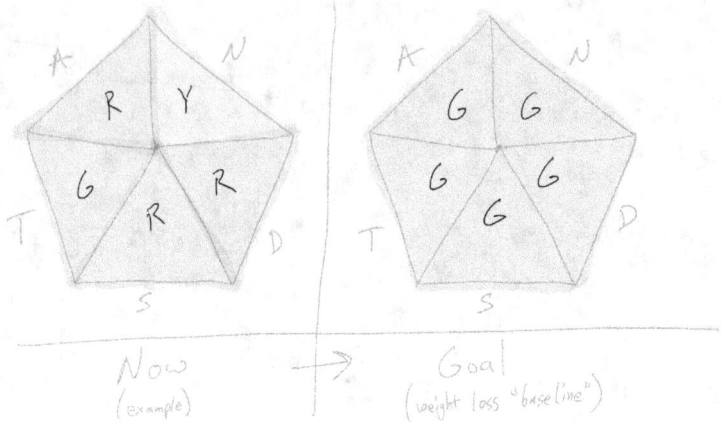

Improve 5 habits.

That's ALL it takes for most people to get lean for life.

The remainder of the book was about HOW to make these habits. So they're easier, more enjoyable, and lasting. You can use the same progression as my clients:

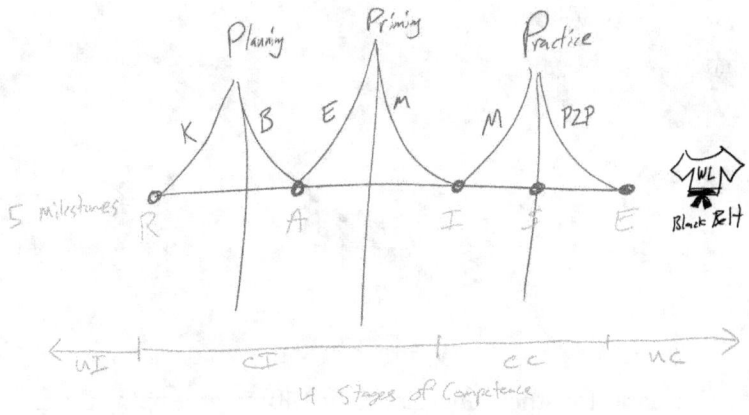

Which boils down to M.A.T.R.R.s of habit:

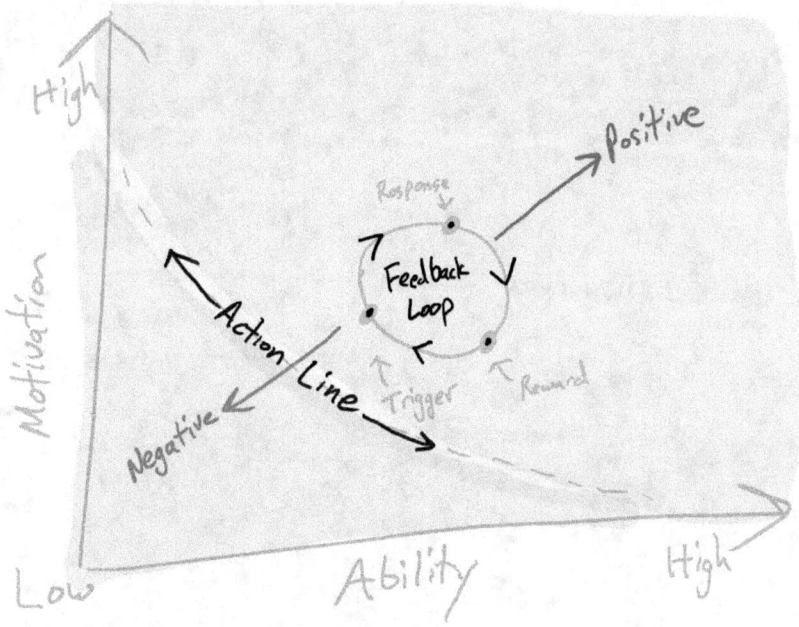

With minor changes/refinements as you turn pain into power:

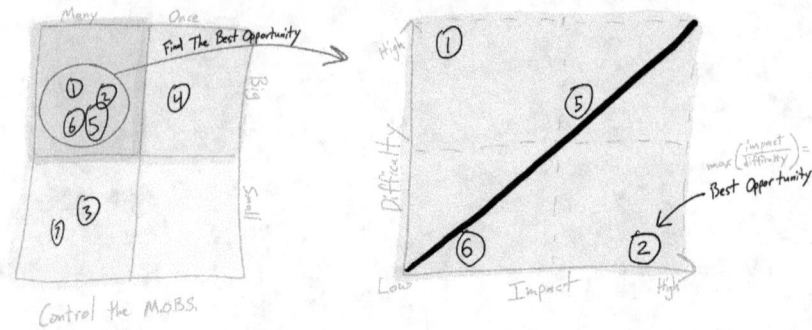

All of this works together synergistically. Ultimately tipping the energy balance scales in your favor:

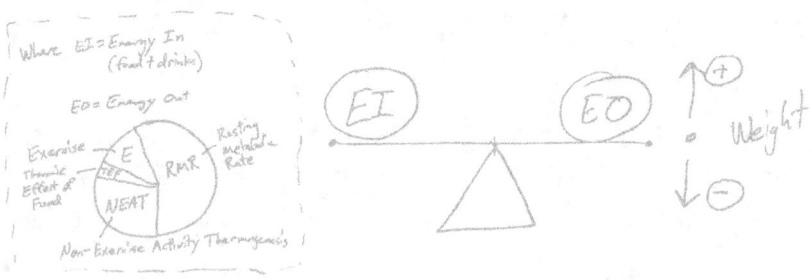

So you can reach your goal:

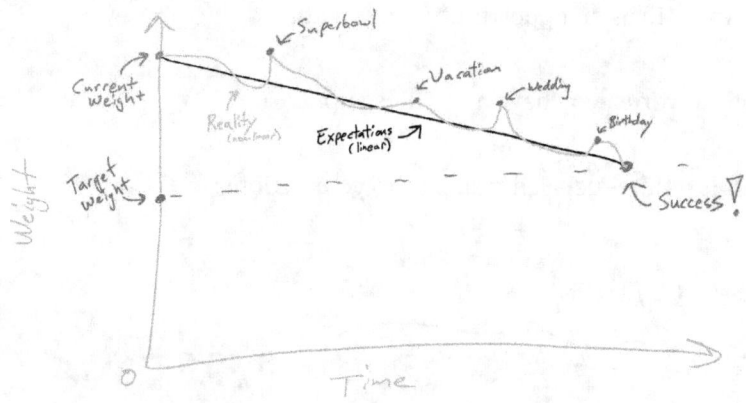

And enjoy a F.R.E.S.H. start once you're lean for life.

Because you know all this & more...

YOUR journey to weight loss mastery will be worlds apart from those who don't:

- Understand weight loss as a SKILL
- Have a blueprint for success
- Optimize for flow
- Remove motivation from the equation
- Trigger the right things at the right times
- Infuse their activities with PERMA
- Use their strengths
- Master their mindware
- Consistently improve their skills
- Leverage positive feedback loops
- Have a system for controlling the M.O.B.S.
- Realize plateaus will happen

Or view pain as an opportunity for growth...

In other words, you have a HUGE leg up.

There's a time-delayed response to your actions:

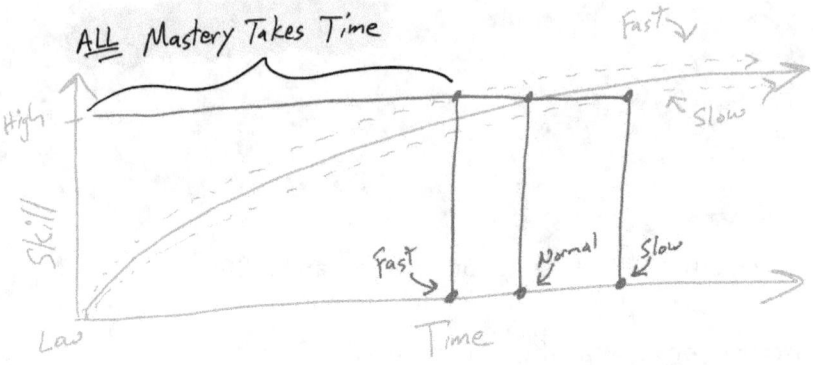

But mastering the basic skills needed to improve your S.T.A.N.D.ing will make & keep you lean for life. Not as fast as the dehydration diets that shed up to 40lbs of water weight in a day...

But as fast as S.A.F.E. & Simply possible.

Some people think this will take years or decades...

But I've seen it done in as little as 6 months.

However long it takes you, I look forward to seeing your results.

And before you begin your metamorphosis, please enjoy 2 parting gifts...

IV

Parting Gifts

54

Old Story, New Meaning

"The greater the difficulty the more glory in surmounting it.
Skillful pilots gain their reputation
from storms and tempests."
–Epictetus

Your success will be like the story of the tortoise and the hare...

With a twist.

Our story starts off in the usual way...

One fine day, a rabbit (new dieter) wants to see what he's made of (realization). So he challenges a turtle (coach) to a race (action).

The turtle accepts, and the race begins.

The rabbit sprints ahead, leaving the turtle in the dust. Then he gets cocky (Dunning-Kruger Effect), and takes a nap (inconsistency).

The turtle keeps moving ahead (M=TIC) until he wins the race.

The rabbit realizes his mistake (stagnation).

And challenges teacher turtle to a rematch.

The turtle accepts, on one condition...

HE gets to choose the course.

The rabbit accepts.

They zip over to the turtle's course.

And the rematch begins (action).

Knowing he can't stop for a nap, the rabbit takes it a little slower this time (improvement). But he's light years ahead.

Victory is certain...

Until he crests the hill.

There, in front of him, is a river too long to circumvent. It goes on far as the eye can see. And just beyond it... is the finish line.

Our hero realizes his mistake.

It would take the rabbit mere minutes to get there if it were solid ground.

But it isn't.

And he can't swim (conscious incompetence).

So he sits there for hours (stagnation). And watches helplessly as the turtle catches up. Slow & steady, the turtle continues down the hill, across the river, and over the finish line.

The sun sets below the horizon.

Cold and alone, our hero sits atop the hill...

Shivering in shame.

"How could I have been so stupid? I thought for sure I'd win!"

The turtle taps him on the shoulder, breaking his dark thoughts.

And invites the rabbit onto his back.

The turtle carries him down the hill, over the water, and into a warm, dry cave for the night.

"Turtle, I want to beat you SO BAD! What can I do?"
   (realization of conscious incompetence)

The turtle looks the rabbit in the eyes.

He looks away.

Thinks for a minute. And says,

"Learn to swim. And try again."

The next day, the rabbit jumps in the water (action).

And almost drowns.
  (flow failure - too much challenge)

He comes back to the turtle,

"I tried to swim, but almost drowned. It was stupid of me to even try. Rabbits can't swim." (fixed mindset - stagnation)

The turtle shakes his head.

"Whether you think you can, or can't, you're right."

Then, he told the rabbit a story about his friend, "Two-toed Thumper." A gold medalist rabbit swimmer who, as you may have guessed, has only 2 toes on one foot.

"But I'm not a natural swimmer like you or two-toed Thumper!"
  (fixed mindset)

"You don't have to be," says the turtle.
  (growth mindset)

"Here, try this instead..."

The turtle gives him a 7-step blueprint for swimming:

  1. Practice floating in shallow water, so you can easily stand up to

breathe

2. Practice coming up for air when floating until you can do it without standing up

3. While floating, practice your strokes and kicks, so you can move forward

4. While breathing, practice streamlining your body for a better glide

5. When you reach this point, you're swimming

6. After you're swimming, practice in deeper and deeper water

7. And the most important rule...

"Practice every day."

(consistency)

"Even if it's just a little. And especially when you don't feel like it. Find something to look forward to, a way to enjoy the process, and get on with it." (M.A.T.R.R.s)

When the rabbit first looked at the plan, he thought it would take FOREVER. (poor mental simulation)

But once he started (action), he found the hours flew by.

(flow & improvement)

He looked forward to practicing every day.

(positive feedback loop).

Until one day, he swam across the river, just for fun.

(evolution)

"OK turtle! Up for another race?"

"Sure!"

They head off to the starting line.

The hare sprints ahead, mindful not to wear himself out. He flies up the hill, down the hill, swims across the river and over the finish line .

He looks back to see the turtle cresting the hill.

He waves to his teacher with a big bunny grin on his face.

The turtle looks down on his pupil with pride.

His eyes tear up.

Stupid bunny grin... hits him in the heart every time. He collects himself. Waves back with his little turtle arm.

And continues on his way.

Most bunnies don't know how to swim. But any bunny can learn.

As the tortoise taught the rabbit...

It's just a M.A.T.R.R. of habit.

55

The Final Gift

I hope you enjoyed the story (*first gift*) as much as I enjoyed writing it.

And that it helps you tie everything together.

The final gift is a set of resources, to help you get the most out of this book. And an invitation — to make your transformation successful beyond your wildest dreams.

Ask, Share & Connect on Facebook

If you would like to:

- Connect with other readers
- Share your feedback / results
- Ask questions

Or just stay on top of my latest projects, join us on Facebook:
www.LeanForLifeBook.com/Facebook/

Additional Bonuses

Yes, I know…

This book is **DENSE.**

The only way to talk about everything is to "chunk" the information into short & sweet acronyms/initializations. So in addition to the bonuses already mentioned:

- Your Free Audiobook
- Weight Loss Limiter Quiz
- Strengths Identifier
- What Successful Dieters Do Differently
- And more…

You'll also find:

- A reference .pdf for acronyms & initializations
- Color photos of images in the book *(for paperback readers)*

With the rest of the bonuses here:
   www.LeanForLifeBook.com/Bonus/

Want Help?

If you want help IMPLEMENTING all the gems in this book, or need someone to be accountable to…

I'm here to help.

Just send an e-mail to:
  Start@LeanForLifeBook.com

Tell me what you're looking for...

And we'll take it from there.

Sincerely,

Nick Ritchey
LIMIT SLAYER